'Round the world cooking library
Scandinavian Cooking

Savory dishes from the four northern sisters: Denmark, Norway, Sweden, Finland

Recipe contributions
by Gunnevi Bonekamp,
Gothenburg, Sweden

International authority on Scandinavian cooking

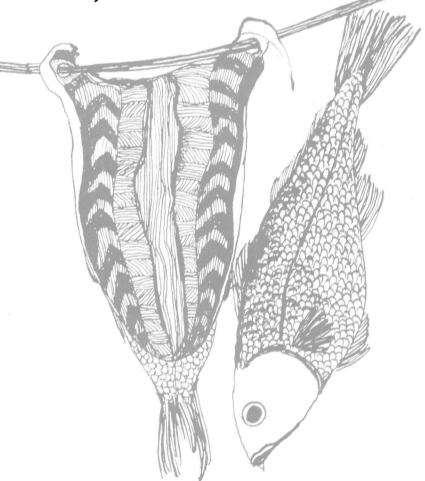

GALAHAD BOOKS • NEW YORK

Contents

Recipe contributions	Gunnevi Bonekamp, home economist to Wezäta Testkitchen, Gothenburg, Sweden; International authority on Scandinavian Cooking.

Editorial staff for 'Round the world cooking library:

Project editor	Wina Born, Dame de la Chaîne des Rôtisseurs and member of the board of the Fédération Internationale de la Presse Gastronomique
Executive editor	Ton van Es
Text editor U.S.A.	Martin Self B.A., J.D.
Photo-edition	Wezäta Testkitchen, Gothenburg, Sweden
Cover photo	Henk van der Heijden, Amsterdam
Design and drawings	Rosemarijn van Limburg Stirum
Created by	Meijer Pers B.V., Amsterdam, The Netherlands
Typeset by	Service Type Inc., Lancaster, Pennsylvania and Internationaal Zetcentrum B.V., Wormerveer, The Netherlands
Printed by	Drukkerij Meijer B.V., Wormerveer, The Netherlands
Bound by	Proost & Brandt N.V., Amsterdam, The Netherlands
Publisher	Drake Publishers Inc., New York, N.Y.
Distributor	Galahad Books, New York, N.Y.

Cup measures in this book are based on an eight ounce cup.

Scandinavia at the table

Denmark, Norway, Sweden and Finland, the four most northerly countries of Europe, are usually pronounced together in one single breath as 'Scandinavia'. But although they do all have very much in common, they are in fact four quite independent countries, three of which are proud monarchies. Earlier in the history of Scandinavia, a kaleidoscope of political combinations once existed: Sweden united with Norway and Denmark, Sweden with Finland, and Denmark with Norway. Thus each country has long had a great influence on the other three. But they have all still retained certain unique and unmistakable characteristics. Scandinavians are tall, blond, good-natured people. They may appear a bit reserved and self-contained at first, but they share an extremely deep love of nature, of silence and solitude. They have a reputation as an easy-going, companionable and hospitable people whose door is always cordially open. Their spare time is usually engaged in outdoor sports; not team sports but recreation in which the individual is alone with nature: skiing on the silent, snow-covered mountain slopes, ice-skating over the cold surface of frozen lakes, canoeing, hiking, fishing and sailing. The long summer evenings in the land of the Midnight Sun are usually spent outdoors, but the long, dark and cold winter is

spent around the warm and cosy open fireplace. (It is no coincidence that the housebound Scandinavians have set a standard of interior decoration and comfortable furniture design that is world renowned.) Getting together with friends to eat and drink the long winter evening away is elevated almost to a ritual in Scandinavia, and nowhere else is there so much imagination, skill and artistry applied to setting the candle laden table.

The real roots of Scandinavian eating lie in the climate. People were forced to stock supplies for the long winter, and in this way the process of preserving meat, fish, vegetables and fruit has been developed into a fine art. Nowhere else in the world can there be found so many different ways of drying, smoking and curing meat and fish. This is a very ancient art: the Vikings who sailed a thousand years ago to Iceland, Greenland and even North America, carried with them smoked meat and dried, salted fish for the long weeks at sea.

But in spite of all the resemblances the Scandinavian countries have with each other, there are still enormous differences, and anyone thoroughly familiar with one country cannot claim familiarity with any of the other three. Centuries of shared history have still left individual characteristics and traditions so different that

each country is quite unique. This is true even in the cooking and dining habits of the four countries. Perhaps this is best revealed in the old saying: 'The Danes live to eat, the Norwegians eat to live, and the Swedes eat to drink'. The Finns are not included so let us complete the saying by adding: '…and the Finns drink to eat'.

4

The gently rolling Danish land-scape, with its green and luscious pastures, is the home of Denmark's dairy herds, famed for their sweet white cream.

Past Copenhagen's famous spiral-steepled City Hall clatter the hoofs of drayhorses, pulling cartloads of foamy Danish lager beer.

Cool Scandinavian fjords provide fishermen with abundant catches.

Codfish lie on racks to dry in the long northern daylight and fresh salty sea breeze.

Denmark

Denmark is Scandinavia's Promised Land, overflowing with milk and honey. Nowhere is the grass greener and thicker and nowhere do the cows give whiter and richer milk and sweeter cream. The vegetable gardens (first planted in the sixteenth century by Dutch, who migrated to Denmark but grew homesick for their familiar fresh green vegetables) produce fresh, tender, young vegetables early in the spring. The orchards yield delicious apples and ripe, sweet cherries (the source of a famous cherry liqueur). Pink, well-fed pigs grunt with satisfaction in this land of natural abundance. In the sea live small red, tasty shrimp and Baltic herring, and in the Limfjord grow large, pearl-colored oysters. Festive eating and drinking are a sturdy tradition in Denmark and every visitor is received in a generous and friendly fashion.

In Danish delicatessens the most inviting and appetizing foods are displayed in overflowing abundance: smoked salmon and eel, cheeses, sausages, ham and the most delicious varieties of fish and game. Eating and drinking are so much a national pastime, that it was not considered out of the ordinary when the late King Frederick appeared on his palace balcony to greet the people of Copenhagen, still wearing his napkin tucked around his neck.

The Danes begin their day with

a breakfast of strong, tasty coffee and delicious sweet coffeerolls, so fine, light and crispy that they have no equal which cannot be anywhere else in the world. Oddly enough, they call these 'Wienerbröd', Viennese rolls, while we know them as the famed Danish pastry. At about one o'clock, time for lunch, the Danes eat their famous 'smörrebröd'. This literally means 'bread spread with butter', but the butter is actually a minor ingredient; in fact, it is not even visible under the three or four layers of delicious garnishes that cover the bread. They make a colorful pattern that delights both the eye and the taste buds – thick slices of smoked fish or meat, ham, hard-boiled or scrambled eggs, mayonnaise, potatoes, horseradish, fruit sauce or compote, cold fish or shellfish, roasted meat, fresh vegetables. Almost anything can go into a smörrebröd, so long as it is colorful in appearance and surprising in taste. One restaurant in Copenhagen has over 200 different varieties of smörrebröd, and they are all deliciously described in a menu more than three feet long! These smörrebröd are prepared to order and flown to many other countries in Western Europe. In the evening, the Danes eat a hearty dinner, a roast with vegetables. The meal usually ends with one of the many sweet combinations of rich cream and fruit for which the Danes are famous.

Beer is the national drink of Denmark, and there are so many different kinds you can choose a different beer for each hour of the day, for each mood and occasion. They range from strong, 'Easter' beers, which contain 8% alcohol, to very light, blond beers to quench a summer thirst. The Danes also love 'akvavit' a crystal-clear, gin-like spirit distilled from potatoes and grain and flavored with caraway seeds. It is usually drunk from small but elegant long-stemmed glasses, so cold that the glass itself becomes fogged. Akvavit must be downed in one large swallow. During the cold, damp Danish winter, people warm their bones with piping hot, strong coffee made even more potent with akvavit. They drop a small shiny coin into the bottom of a coffee cup, pour in enough black coffee to make the coin disappear, and then pour in enough akvavit to make the coin visible again, gleaming in the bottom of the cup.

Norway

Nature blessed Norway with an overflowing abundance of mountains, rocky shores, fjords and virgin forests. It is the perfect place to enjoy fully the wonders of nature, but a hard place to live, and only about 4% of the land can be cultivated. Norwegian cooking, therefore, is not very rich, but rather simple and hearty. Cooking depends heavily on two staples: fish and potatoes. In this land of endless coastlines, fjords and mountain streams, herring and cod, turbot and sole, and salmon and trout are among the best to be found anywhere in the world. And they are all so attractively fresh, being bought while still alive, that most Norwegians consider fish eaten anywhere outside of Norway never fresh enough for their taste. Norwegians have also discovered many ways to preserve their fish and their scarce supply of meat for long periods. Especially in the islands of the north and along the fjords, you can see long horizontal bars hung with large pieces of cod to dry in the ice-cold, bone-dry, north wind. After two or three months, the cod is dry and as hard as a rock. It can be kept for years without going bad. Sometimes, cod is salted and then placed on rocks to dry. Norwegians call this 'klippfisk'. Norwegian housewives make a special dish called 'lutfisk' from the salted dry cod. This is done by soaking the cod for a few days in fresh water and then putting it in a mixture of water and birchwood ash so that it acquires a slightly rubbery consistency.

Norwegians are very fond of this dish but to non-Scandinavians it seems on the bland side and must be garnished with healthy amounts of butter, cream and mustard to become really delectable.

After the autumn slaughter, (there is not enough forage to keep animals through the winter) mutton is salted and smoked or hung out in the cold, freezing Norwegian wind as much as six months. After this curing process, it remains edible for years. (In the folklore museum at Oslo, there are legs of mutton preserved in this way that are said to be at least three hundred years old and still edible.)

To the list of delicious gastronomic specialities of Norway, knowledgeable gourmets add the royal salmon, the snow grouse and such game as elk, hare and, above all, reindeer. A tender reindeer steak, fried in good country butter and accompanied by a compote of woodland berries, is one of the most delectable dishes that can be had anywhere in Scandinavia.

On many remote Norwegian farms, women still bake their own bread, and there is a vigorous spirit of competition between farmwives as to whose 'flattbröd' is the thinnest and the crispiest. This dark crisp bread is the perfect companion not only for smoked reindeer but also for another Norwegian speciality: 'Gjetöst', a cheese made from goat's milk that has been simmered so long that it acquires a rust-brown, caramel color and a slightly sweet taste. Breakfast in Norway is an extensive affair. The tourist staying in his first Norwegian hotel will be surprised to find such a fabulously laid-out table decked with numerous sorts of cold meat and fish, cheese, eggs, jam, compotes and at least five different types of bread. Everyone can choose what he likes and as much as he likes. Cordial, blond waitresses serve hot coffee with milk. After such a breakfast Norwegians are understandably not very hungry at lunchtime, and they usually simply have a sandwich and a glass of milk. Early in the evening the members of the family gather around the large dinner table, on which, more often than not, fish is the special treat.

The Baltic Sea is renowned for a small but delectable herring found nowhere else. For centuries Swedish housewives have used this fish in preparing the most delicious dishes, soaking the her- *ring in sweet and spicy sauces or in velvety smooth ones made from sweet and sour creams. Added to these are fresh green herbs, and particularly dill is a must.*

SweСden

'Rich Sweden' is a phrase often used enviously by the rest of Europe to describe this Scandinavian country. Its wealth and prosperity are displayed in the most enticing fashion in the Swedish 'Smörgåsbord'. Smörgåsbord is also found in the other countries of Scandinavia, but it is never so abundant as in Sweden. It developed from a time when each guest at big country gatherings brought some food of his own. Today it is an immeasurably grander affair. With his plate in hand the guest serves himself from the richly laid out buffet, selecting just what he wants. This sort of meal reveals two very Swedish characteristics: first, their hearty appetites – each person can spoon out as much as he likes as often he pleases – and second, Swedish individualism – everyone chooses his own place to enjoy the food, even alone in a corner if he feels like it. The most elaborate smörgåsbord can be found in

From the countryside – Finland's well known Karelian pies, together with pickles, ham and the familiar home-made beer in a barrel.

Finns like their crayfish seasoned with dill.

Summer in Scandinavia is brief but intense, with daylight hours that hardly seem to end and a sun that rises almost as soon as it has set. During this bright northern summer Scandinavians live out-doors as much as they can, hardly seeming to take time even to sleep. They dance around the May Pole and Midsummer Night bonfires, picnic and walk and swim under the never darkening sky. And at the famous Tivoli amusement park in Copenhagen, colorful fireworks light up those very few hours between sunset and sunrise.

Finland

the luxury restaurants of Stockholm, Operakällaren and Stalmestergarden, where more than 60 different dishes are displayed on a beautifully decorated buffet table. But it would be wrong to think that you can just choose at random from the assortment. Quite the contrary! Everything is displayed together, but the guests follow certain unwritten rules. Everyone invariably begins with herring. Delectable Baltic herring take on a variety of shapes, forms and flavors: they can be marinated, smoked, sour, sweet-and-sour, in cream sauce, in piquant sauce, and on and on. After this, each person takes a clean plate and goes on to the second course, which consists of cold fish: salmon or trout or some other fish prepared in aspic and ideally served with a cucumber salad. Then comes the cold-meat course: liver pâtés, roast beef, pork, and sometimes delicacies such as smoked reindeer or other cold game. This is accompanied by a green salad with sour cream or a potato salad with a sweet-and-sour sauce of such woodland delights as bilberries, cloudberries or cranberries. Then it is time to begin dishing out surprises from the containers kept warm over a fondue burner. There are meatballs in gravy, spicy ragouts, sometimes even stewed bear or reindeer and often warm omelets or soufflés. Afterwards

come cheeses, and finally dessert or fruit salad. With a smörgåsbord the natural drink is akvavit, brandy or beer. The guest pours his own drinks, sometimes from small decanters which stand on the buffet table, the akvavit from bottles frozen into blocks of ice. Toasting with akvavit is a ritual with fixed rules in Sweden. At very formal dinners you take the glass in the right hand (men hold their glasses just above the top button of their jackets), look the person to whom the toast is directed in the eye and say 'skål', bowing your head and emptying the glass in one swallow. Then you look each other in the eye again, in a little less solemn and more friendly way than before, nod and put the glass down.

Finland is a mysterious country of deep solitude, of light, opal-colored summer nights and hard, cold, bitter and dark winters, and of 60,000 lakes that sparkle among somber, green forests of fir trees. Strictly speaking the Finns are not really Scandinavians. Their origins lie somewhere in the faraway steppes of Central Asia and their unpronounceable language is a reminder of their distant and misty past. They are above all the people of the sauna. The sauna is the pivot around which Finnish life turns, and even the Finnish Cabinet has been known to meet in one. A sauna bath (in which you sit in a small, smotheringly hot room with pine-wood walls, where the temperature can rise to 225° to 250°, rubbing yourself with a stiff brush and soap and then going under a cold shower or for a swim in a cold lake) is a favorite pastime and way of relaxing, and it is often the central event of a social gathering. People invite their friends out for a sauna party, and the most enjoyable part is the 'after-sauna'. They relax either outdoors in front of the log cabin along the banks of a lake, or in an easy-chair in the living room before an open fire. After a sauna it is guaranteed that you will become very hungry and thirsty, and the Finns love to eat and drink together afterwards to replenish themselves.

Finnish food is food for people with simple taste and keen appetites. It is at its best prepared in a straightforward and simple manner: splendid fresh trout and other fish from the lakes, slipped onto branches and roasted over an open fire; delicious Lapland salmon bound to planks and smoked before a fire; priceless fresh burbot caviar; the endless variety of mushrooms found in the woods that taste so delicious with sour cream; wild summer berries such as orange-red arctic brambleberries, and raspberries that have grown large and sweet and have soaked up the aroma of the bright Lapland summer nights.
The great party-time in Finland comes in August, at the opening of the crayfish season.
Everywhere in Finland crayfish parties are organized, and heaps of these tiny, lobster-like creatures, boiled until fiery-red in richly spiced dill bouillon, are washed down with vodka. That akvavit is less popular in Finland than vodka is only one of the many signs of the century the country spent under Russian rule. Some of the best features of Finnish cooking are the result of a unique blend of Russian and Scandinavian influences.

ATLANTIC OCEAN

LOFOTEN

LAPLAND

RUSSIA

NORWAY

SWEDEN

FINLAND

OSLO

STAVANGER

STOCKHOLM

HELSINKI

THE BALTIC SEA

NORTH SEA

GÖTEBORG

DENMARK

COPENHAGEN
MALMÖ

GERMANY

Danish open sandwiches

Open sandwiches are a Danish national institution. The Danes call these sandwiches simply 'smörrebröd', literally, bread and butter, but anyone who has tried any of these artfully arranged sandwiches will know that three or four pieces of smörrebröd are more than enough to make an elaborate and filling meal. Danish restaurants have menus in which the diner can choose from literally hundreds of different types of smörrebröd. The choice is often baffling – there are, for example, over 20 different possible variations of 'smörrebröd med ryer', simply open sandwiches with baby shrimp.

Open sandwiches in a somewhat simpler form (but no less fancifully created) are taken to work at the office for lunch and children carry them to school in a small tin lunch box, with 'eat heartily' often inscribed on the top. Smörrebröd are also perfect for picnics.

Danish beer, exported to almost every country in the world, goes perfectly with smörrebröd. The Danes often drink their beer accompanied by a glass of 'akvavit', a clear, innocent looking fluid, but a drink to be treated with respect. Akvavit is drunk from thimble-sized, long-stemmed glasses filled to the brim. First the sweet but strong akvavit, and then a swallow of beer – the perfect combination with smörrebröd!

Smörrebröd

Smorrebrod—breads

There is no more pleasant experience in eating than picking-and-choosing from the fantastic variety of small, beautiful and marvelously tasty sandwiches known as smorrebrod. They turn up as a first course, as a lunch, or, as the Danes like, in a full course meal—first fish, then meat and/or salad, then cheese. Both the art and the fun of making open sandwiches is variety—variety of color, flavor, texture. For you don't really make your sandwich— you compose it, as an artist plans a picture. First the base— and for that you need a variety of breads—thin-sliced, crust-trimmed, white, light rye, dark pumpernickel, Knackebrod or Rye-krisp, light and dark, too. Think about taste when you choose your bread. White for gentle flavors—fish, chicken, mild cheese. Light rye for strong fish or full-flavored meat. Dark rye for spicy, well-seasoned mixtures. Spread base lightly with sweet butter, anchovy butter, herb butter, parsley butter. Next a lettuce leaf, or a thick covering of finely snipped parsley or chervil; cucumber slices, paper-thin; thin-sliced apple—let your fancy be your guide. Shapes? Squares, oblongs, fan-shaped, triangles, circles—any shape you fancy— and your cutters—dictate.

Smörrebröd med fisk

Smorrebrod with fish

Thin bread, thickly spread with seasoned butter, lettuce, thin-sliced cucumber, tomatoes, potatoes, topped with—

Herring, marinated in wine sauce, cream sauce, or fried. Marinated or jellied eel. Smoked eel with mayonnaise or horseradish whipped cream. Thin-sliced smoked salmon roll, filled with horseradish whipped cream. Scrambled eggs topped with sliced smoked salmon. Anchovy fillets with sliced hard-cooked eggs. Herring tidbits with tomato and egg slices. Herring salad with sliced cucumber rings. Baby shrimp with mayonnaise, served separately. Cold fried fish with sauce remoulade or sauce tartare. Sardines with tomato sauce. Crab salad topped with sliced egg and tomatoes. Crab with sliced egg and asparagus tips.

Smörrebröd med köd

Smörrebröd med salat

Smorrebrod with meat

Again the base is important—
thin bread or crisp-bread
spread with butter well seasoned
with mustard, anchovy, parsley;
thin-sliced cucumber, apple or
onions, finely chopped, parsley
or chervil, so thick the bread
cannot be seen. Now to build
your sandwich . . .

Slices of ham, wedges of
apple, stewed prunes.

Rolled sliced ham filled with
herb or horseradish
mayonnaise and chopped egg.

Ham with sliced pineapple
and banana and sweetened
mayonnaise.

Ham with scrambled egg
and chives.

Ham with chopped egg,
topped with chopped chives.

Raw ground beef with fried
egg and chopped chives.

Raw ground beef mixed with
raw egg yolk and chopped
pickles.

Sliced roast beef, tongue, or
braised veal or pork roll rolled
around asparagus tips.

Italian salad, pickled
mushrooms or sliced tomatoes
with horseradish mayonnaise.

Sliced liverwurst with sweet
and sour pickles, cucumber
slices, crisp fried bacon or
sliced egg.

Smorrebrod with salad

Thin bread, spread with
seasoned butter, then a mound of:

Cold lamb salad, sliced
cucumbers and parsley.

Chicken salad, sliced egg and
a cherry tomato.

Egg salad, topped with rolled,
thinly sliced salami.

Lobster salad topped with
mayonnaise and sprinkled
with chopped pistachio nuts.

Now take a look at your works
of art. Is there room for a bit of
parsley? A cherry tomato?
A cauliflower floweret? A radish
or carrot curl, a flourish of
chopped chives, parsley, or
bacon bits, a sprig of dill, a
tomato wedge, strips of green
or red pepper, sliced olives,
onion rings.

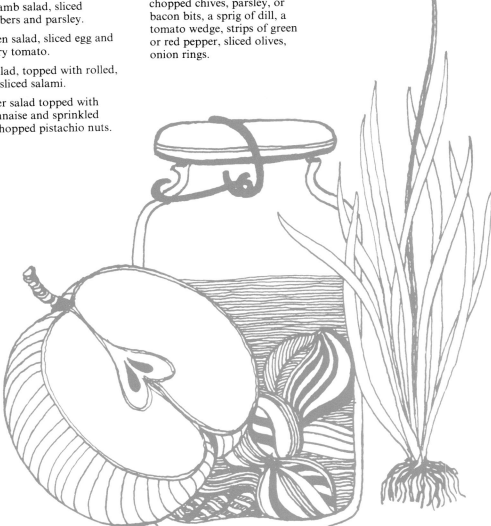

Leverpostej

Danish liver paté

10 servings

4 tablespoons margarine or
  butter
½ cup flour
1 cup milk
1 pound beef liver
½ pound salt pork
1 large onion
1 egg
1 teaspoon salt
¼ teaspoon black pepper

Melt margarine in small
saucepan; blend in flour.
Gradually add milk, stirring
briskly until smooth. Cook over
medium heat stirring constantly
until thick and bubbly; cool.
Cut liver, pork and onion into
small pieces. Puree in small
amounts in blender at high
speed or put through food
grinder. Stir pureed mixture into
white sauce; blend well. Add
egg, salt and pepper; mix well.
Pour into a well buttered
9″ × 5″ × 3″ baking dish.
Cover top with foil, sealing
edges tightly. Place in large
baking pan. Pour boiling water
into baking pan to a depth of
2″. Bake in a 350° oven 1 hour.
Remove from oven and lift
off cover. Cool. Store covered
in refrigerator. Serve in ½″ slices.

Smörrebröd
H. C. Andersen

Hans Christian Andersen
sandwich

4 servings

4 slices rye or pumpernickel
  bread
  Margarine or butter
4 slices liver paté page 15 or
8 slices liverwurst
1 tomato, sliced
8 cooked bacon curls
4 pickles, cut into fans
  Lettuce leaves

Spread bread generously with
margarine; top with liver paté.
Garnish with tomato, bacon
curls and pickles. Serve on
lettuce leaves.

Smörrebröd Oliver Twist

Oliver Twist sandwich

6 servings

6 slices pumpernickel bread
  Margarine or butter
6 slices cooked ham
1 tablespoon horseradish
½ cup whipped cream or
½ cup sour cream
12 cooked pitted prunes
6 orange slices

Spread bread with margarine.
Place folded slice of ham on
bread. Stir horseradish into
whipped cream. Heap spoonful
of cream in center of ham.
Place a prune on either side of
cream. Cut orange slices halfway
and twist; place in center of
cream. Serve immediately.

Looking like a brilliant abstract painting, this collection of containers and jars holds an almost limitless variety of appetizing Scandinavian seafood delicacies.

17

People the world over have heard
of the Swedish smörgåsbord. In
fact, the other countries of
Scandinavia also enjoy this buffet
table on which a choice of
delicious dishes are displayed.
But in Sweden, the smörgåsbord
appears in its richest and most
elaborate form. From a festively
laid table, each person can choose
from the best the land and sea
have to offer. First fish dishes,
then salads, then both cold and
hot meat and pâtés, and finally
cheese or a fruit compote.
Of all the endless variations
brought to the table, the most
elaborate come with the fish
dishes. The 'sillbord', an
enormous choice of seafood
delicacies with herring as their
basis, is a Swedish discovery (or
at least so declare the Swedes
with pride). The fish is
marinated, salted, fried, smoked
and often find a place in salads.
The hospitable Swedes want
everyone to enjoy something from
the inexhaustible riches of the
sea. And nothing tastes better
with this sillbord than a good
glass of Swedish akvavit.

Hors d'oeuvres

Sildcocktail

Herring cocktail

6 servings

- 6 *lettuce leaves*
- 3 *cooked, cold potatoes, peeled and sliced*
- 1 *(5½ ounce) can pickled matjes herring fillets*
- 4 *tablespoons mayonnaise*
- 2 *tablespoons chopped dill or chives*

Place lettuce leaves in small bowls or sherbet cups. Arrange sliced potatoes on lettuce leaf. Slice herring fillets; arrange over potatoes. Garnish each cocktail with mayonnaise. Sprinkle chopped dill or chives over mayonnaise. Serve cold.

Sherrysill

Herring in sherry pickle

4 servings

- 2 *salted schmalz herring, filleted and skinned*
- ⅓ *cup sherry wine*
- ¼ *cup water*
- 3 *tablespoons vinegar*
- ½ *cup sugar*
- ¼ *teaspoon ground allspice or*
- 3 *allspice berries, crushed*
- 2 *onions, thinly sliced*
  Chopped fresh dill

Cover herring with cold water; soak 24 hours. Drain and rinse. Place in a non-metallic bowl. Combine sherry, water, vinegar, sugar and allspice; pour over herring. Refrigerate about 24 hours. Serve garnished with sliced onions and dill.

Inlagd sild

Danish pickled salted herring

4 servings

- 2 *salted schmalz herring, filleted and skinned*
- 2 *medium onions, sliced*
- ½ *cup vinegar*
- ⅔ *cup water*
- 1 *cup sugar*
- 10 *allspice berries, crushed*

Cover fillets with cold water; soak 24 hours. Drain and rinse; cut into ½" pieces. Place in non-metallic bowl or glass jar. Combine remaining ingredients and bring to a boil; cool; pour over herring. Refrigerate several hours or overnight before serving.

Etikkasilliä

Finnish pickled herring

4 servings

- 4 *salted herring, filleted and skinned*
- 2 *cups vinegar*
- 1 *cup water*
- ½ *cup sugar*
- 3 *bay leaves*
- 1 *2" piece ginger root, sliced thinly*
- 2 *teaspoons mustard seed*
- 1 *tablespoon prepared horseradish*
- 4 *small red onions, thinly sliced*
- 1 *carrot, thinly sliced*

Soak herring in cold water at least 24 hours in a cool place. Drain; cut into ½" strips. Combine vinegar, water and sugar; bring to a boil over moderate heat. Simmer about 5 minutes until syrupy. In a non-metallic bowl, make alternate layers of herring, bay leaves, ginger root, mustard seed, horseradish, sliced onions and carrots. Pour vinegar syrup over fish; cover; refrigerate for 3 days.

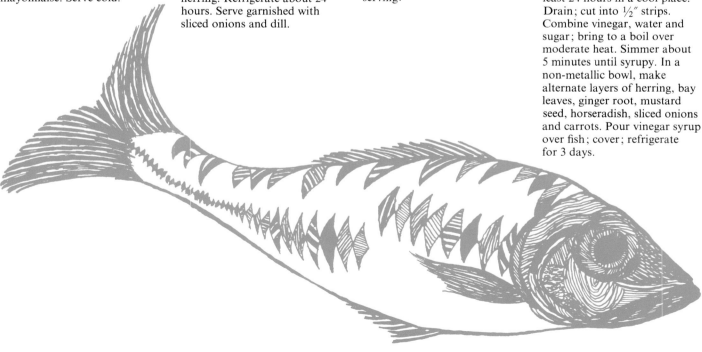

Gravad sild

Danish marinated herring

4 servings

> 4 herring or trout, about
>   6-ounces each
> 4 tablespoons dill weed
> 6 tablespoons vegetable oil
> ⅔ cup vinegar
> 2 teaspoons salt
> 1 tablespoon sugar
> ½ teaspoon ground white
>   pepper
> 1 teaspoon dry mustard

Fillet fish and remove skin.
Place alternate layers of fish and
dill in a non-metallic bowl.
Combine and beat with a fork
oil, vinegar, salt, sugar, pepper
and mustard; pour over fish.
Cover bowl; refrigerate for
several hours or overnight.

Sildgratin

Danish herring au gratin

6 servings

> 2 schmalz or matjes herring
>   fillets
> 4 tablespoons margarine or
>   butter
> 1 tablespoon chopped onion
> 3 tablespoons flour
> 2 cups half-and-half
> ½ teaspoon salt
> ¼ teaspoon ground white pepper
> 2 tablespoons chopped parsley
> 6 small cooked potatoes,
>   peeled and sliced
> 2 hard cooked eggs, chopped
> 2 tablespoons grated Parmesan
>   cheese
> 1 tablespoon margarine or
>   butter

Soak fillets in cold water for
24 hours; drain. Cut fillets into
½"strips. Melt margarine
in saucepan, add onion and cook
until transparent. Stir in flour;
remove from heat; gradually
add half-and-half. Cook over
medium heat, stirring constantly,
until mixture comes to a boil
and is thickened. Stir in salt,
pepper and parsley. Butter
6 individual casserole dishes;
arrange 1 sliced potato in
bottom of each, cover with half
the sauce. Divide chopped egg
and herring evenly among the
casseroles, top with remaining
sauce. Sprinkle with Parmesan
cheese; dot with margarine.
Bake in very hot oven (450°)
about 15 minutes, or until
bubbly and top is lightly
browned.

Rosolli

Finnish herring salad

4 to 6 servings

> 1 salted regular or schmalz
>   herring (about 1 pound)
> ½ cup whipped cream
> 1 tablespoon pickled beet juice
> ½ teaspoon sugar
> 1 teaspoon vinegar
> 2 cups cold, cooked potatoes,
>   coarsely diced
> 2 cups cold, cooked carrots,
>   coarsely diced
> 1 (1 pound) can beets, drained
>   and coarsely diced
> 2 medium, tart apples, peeled,
>   cored and diced
> 1 large pickle, coarsely diced
> 2 hard cooked eggs, coarsely
>   chopped
> ½ tablespoon finely chopped
>   onion
>   Parsley or watercress sprigs

Soak herring in cold water for
24 hours; skin and fillet.
Combine whipped cream, beet
juice, sugar and vinegar; chill.
Cut herring into cubes; combine
with remaining ingredients,
except parsley; mix well. Fold in
whipped cream dressing. Chill.
Serve garnished with parsley or
watercress.

Sillpudding

Herring pudding

4 to 6 servings

> 1 salted regular or schmalz
>   herring (about ¾ to 1 pound)
> 2 tablespoons margarine or
>   butter
> 1½ cups thinly sliced onion
> 3 cups cooked potatoes,
>   peeled and sliced
> ¼ teaspoon ground white pepper
> 2 eggs
> 2 tablespoons flour
> 1¾ cups milk

Soak herring in cold water 24
hours; skin and fillet; cut into
½" strips. Melt margarine in
large skillet, add onions and
cook until transparent, stirring
occasionally. Add potatoes;
cook, stirring occasionally,
until heated through, about 10
minutes. Place half the potatoes
and onion mixture in bottom of
greased 9 inch round (2 inches
high) baking pan. Arrange
herring pieces over potatoes,
sprinkle with pepper; cover
with remaining potato mixture.
Combine eggs, flour and milk;
beat until just blended, not
foamy; pour over potatoes.
Place pan in larger baking pan.
Pour boiling water in outside
pan to a depth of 1" on
smaller pan. Bake in a hot oven
(425°) until top is browned and
custard is set, about 30 to 40
minutes. Serve hot.

Joppe's shrimp salad. Denmark's small delicate shrimp have a sweet and salty taste. They are so delicious that no gourmet would ever think of covering them with mayonnaise.

Joppes räksallad

Joppe's shrimp salad

4 servings

   1 *pound shrimp, cooked and peeled*
2½ *cups sliced fresh mushrooms*
   2 *medium tomatoes, sliced*
   1 *(8½ ounce) can asparagus spears, drained*
   1 *cup peas, cooked*
   2 *tablespoons oil*
   2 *teaspoons vinegar*
½ *teaspoon salt*
¼ *teaspoon dill weed*
   2 *hard cooked eggs, cut in wedges*

Arrange shrimp, mushrooms, tomatoes, asparagus and peas in salad bowl. Combine oil, vinegar, salt and dill; pour over salad mixture. Garnish with egg wedges.

Sildsalat

Gravad lax

Danish herring salad

6 servings

   2   salted regular or schmalz herring
   3   medium cooked potatoes, peeled and diced
   2   small cooked or canned beets, diced
   1   large pickle, diced
   2   medium tart apples, peeled, cored and diced
   ½   cup cooked ham, tongue or corned beef, diced
   2   tablespoons finely chopped onion
   2   tablespoons margarine or butter
   2   tablespoons flour
   1¼ cups half-and-half
   1   tablespoon vinegar
   1   teaspoon prepared mustard
   ½   teaspoon salt
        Pinch of sugar

Soak herring overnight in cold water; skin and fillet. Cut herring into ½″ pieces. Combine with potatoes, beets, pickle, apple, meat and onion. Chill. Melt margarine in saucepan; stir in flour. Remove from heat; stir in half-and-half, vinegar, mustard, salt and sugar. Cook over medium heat, stirring constantly, until mixture comes to a boil and is thickened. Carefully stir into salad mixture; chill. Serve on lettuce, garnished with hard-cooked egg slices, if desired.

Swedish marinated salmon

6 servings

   2   tablespoons salt
   2   tablespoons sugar
   1   tablespoon peppercorns, crushed
   1   pound salmon, cut into 2 fillets
   1   large bunch fresh dill, chopped coarsely

Combine salt, sugar and peppercorns. Place fish on large piece heavy duty foil. Cover fish with dill; sprinkle with salt mixture. Top with second fish fillet. Close foil securely; place on dish or tray. Pile several weights or 3 or 4 cans of food on foil packet. Refrigerate at least 48 hours turning packet several times. Be sure to keep weights on packet. Remove fish; scrape off seasonings. Slice thinly and serve with salmon sauce (recipe page 30, 3rd column).

Västkustsallad

Swedish Westcoast salad

4 servings

   1 (6½ ounce) can lobster
   1 (10 ounce) can whole
   clams, drained
   1 cup cooked shrimp, peeled
   1 (3 ounce) can sliced
   mushrooms
   ¼ cup mayonnaise
   ¼ cup sour cream
   1 tablespoon lemon juice
   ½–1 teaspoon salt
   Lettuce leaves
   2 tomatoes, quartered

Drain lobster and remove
membranes. Combine lobster,
clams, shrimp, mushrooms,
mayonnaise, sour cream, lemon
juice and salt; toss lightly until
mixed. Arrange salad on lettuce
leaves. Garnish with tomato
wedges.

Krabbsallad

Swedish crab salad

4 servings

   1 (6½ ounce) can crabmeat
   2 stalks celery, chopped
   1 teaspoon grated onion
   1–2 tablespoons lemon juice
   ¼ teaspoon dill weed
   ½ cup sour cream
   Freshly ground black pepper
   Lettuce leaves

Drain crabmeat and remove
membranes. Combine crabmeat
celery, onion, lemon juice, dill,
sour cream, and pepper. Toss
lightly; arrange salad on lettuce.

Hummersalat

Danish curried lobster salad

4 servings

   1 (6½ ounce) can lobster
   ¼ cup mayonnaise
   ¼ cup sour cream
   1 teaspoon lemon juice
   ½ teaspoon curry powder
   2 stalks celery, chopped
   1 apple, cored and diced
   Lettuce leaves
   2 hard cooked eggs, quartered

Drain lobster and remove
membranes. Combine
mayonnaise, sour cream, lemon
juice and curry; blend until
smooth. Add celery, apple and
mayonnaise mixture to lobster;
toss lightly. Pile salad lightly in
lettuce leaves; garnish with
egg wedges.

Solöga

Swedish sun's eye

1 serving

   1 egg yolk
   1 tablespoon chopped
   Bermuda or red onion
   6 anchovy fillets, chopped

Place egg yolk in center of a
salad plate. Surround with
a circle of chopped onion, then a
circle of chopped anchovies.
To eat: stir all together and
spread on toast. (Mixture may
also be lightly fried in butter,
then spread on toast.)

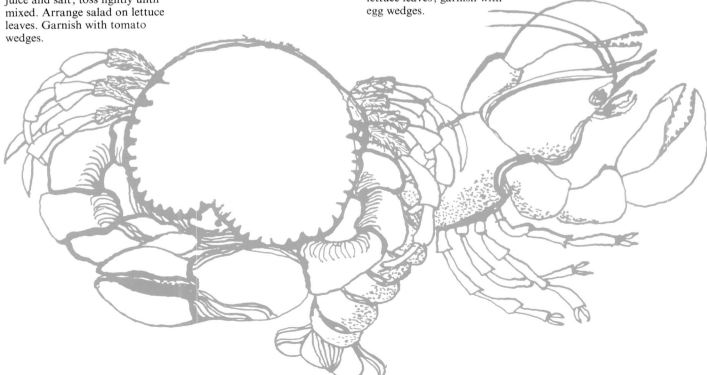

Fisksalat

Danish fish salad

4 servings

  ½ *cup mayonnaise*
  2 *teaspoons prepared mustard*
  2 *tablespoons lemon juice*
  ¾ *pound cooked, flaked cod or*
     other white fish
     Lettuce leaves
  1 *hard cooked egg, sliced*
     Watercress or dill

Combine mayonnaise, mustard
and lemon juice. Carefully stir in
flaked fish; chill. Serve on
lettuce leaves; garnish with
hard-cooked egg slices and
watercress or dill.

Tomater med fyld

Danish stuffed tomatoes

6 servings

  1 *(1 pound) jar pickled*
     schmalz herring
  2 *tart apples, peeled, cored*
     and diced
  ½ *cup mayonnaise*
 1½ *teaspoons dried dill weed*
  ¼ *teaspoon salt*
  ⅛ *teaspoon ground white pepper*
  2 *tablespoons cream or*
     half-and-half
  6 *medium tomatoes*
     Parsley or dill sprigs

Drain herring; chop. Combine
herring, apple, mayonnaise, dill
weed, salt, pepper and cream.
Remove stem end from
tomatoes; carefully remove
seeds and juice. Fill tomatoes
with herring salad mixture.
Serve cold, garnished with
sprig of parsley or dill.

Hjemmelavet kaviar

Danish caviar

    Danish caviar
    Lemon wedges
    Chopped onion
    Chopped egg
    Sour cream
    Butter
    Pumpernickel bread
    Hot toast

Serve caviar in a bowl of ice.
Surround caviar with lemon
wedges, chopped onion,
chopped egg, sour cream and
butter all in separate bowls or
serving dishes. Place bread and
toast in serving dishes or
baskets. Serve chilled aquavit,
vodka or champagne, if desired.

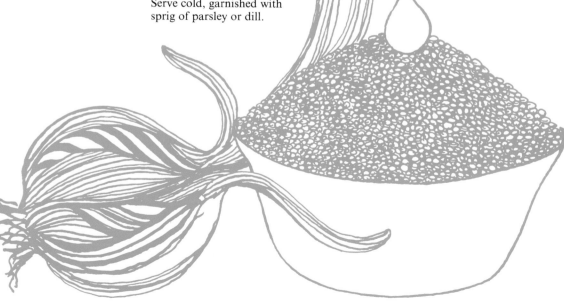

Soups

Danish pea soup

Swedish spinach soup

Swedish meat soup

Köttsoppa

Swedish meat soup

6 servings

- 2 *pounds soup meat*
- 3 *quarts water*
- 2 *medium carrots, coarsely diced*
- 1 *turnip, cut into ½" cubes*
- 1 *stalk celery, diced*
- 1 *medium onion, spiked with 2 cloves*
- 2 *scallions or leeks, sliced*
- 2 *teaspoons salt*
- 1 *teaspoon white pepper*

Place meat in large saucepan; add water. Bring to a boil; skim. Add salt; reduce heat and simmer about 2 hours. Add carrot, turnip, celery, onion and scallions; sprinkle with salt and pepper. Bring to a boil again; reduce heat and simmer 1 hour. Remove meat, cut into pieces, return to soup and heat thoroughly.

Spenatsoppa

Swedish spinach soup

4 servings

- 1 *(10½ ounce) can cream of chicken soup*
- 1 *cup milk*
- 2 *cups boiling water*
- 2 *chicken bouillon cubes*
- 1 *(10 ounce) package frozen chopped spinach, thawed*
- 1 *teaspoon salt*
- ¼ *teaspoon pepper*
- 2 *tablespoons chopped parsley*
- 2 *hard-cooked eggs*

In a large saucepan, combine soup, milk, and boiling water in which bouillon cubes have been dissolved. Add spinach. Place mixture in blender for a few seconds on medium speed just until spinach is very finely chopped; do not puree. Return to saucepan; simmer 10 minutes. Add salt and pepper. Garnish with chopped parsley and quarters of hard-cooked eggs.

Gule aerter

Danish pea soup

6 to 8 servings

- ¾ *pound dried yellow peas*
- 8 *cups water*
- 1 *(¾ to 1 pound) smoked pork shoulder, cut into small pieces*
- 1 *carrot, diced*
- 1 *medium onion, chopped*
- ¼ *teaspoon dried marjoram*
- 1 *teaspoon ginger*
- 1½ *teaspoons salt*

Soak peas in water about 12 hours, unless peas are quick-cooking variety. In a large saucepan, bring peas to a boil in the same water; skim. Add meat, carrot, onion and seasonings. Cover and simmer slowly about 1½ hours or until peas are tender. Season to taste.

Fiskesuppe

Norwegian fish soup

4 servings

- 2 *tablespoons margarine or butter*
- 2 *leeks or scallions, sliced*
- 4 *medium potatoes, diced*
- 1 *stalk celery, diced*
- 2 *teaspoons salt*
- 1 *teaspoon black pepper*
- 5 *cups water*
- 1 *pound fresh or frozen fish fillets*
- 1 *tablespoon chopped fresh dill or*
- 1 *teaspoon dried dill*

In a large, heavy skillet melt margarine; saute leeks, potatoes and celery about 5 minutes over low heat. Add salt, pepper, and water; bring to a boil and cook about 10 to 15 minutes or until vegetables are tender. Cut fish fillets into 1-inch pieces; add to soup about 10 minutes before vegetables are tender. Correct seasoning and sprinkle with dill. Serve immediately.

Norrländsk laxsoppa

Norrlandsk salmon soup

4 servings

> 5 cups liquid (drain liquid
> from can of salmon; add
> water to make 5 cups)
> 3 tablespoons barley
> 2 medium carrots, diced
> 1 medium turnip, diced
> 1 medium onion, chopped
> 1 (16-ounce) can pink salmon
> 1 teaspoon salt
> Dash black pepper
> 2 tablespoons chopped parsley

Bring salmon liquid and water
to a boil. Add barley, boil 30
minutes. Add vegetables and
cook for 10–15 minutes, or until
tender. Add salmon pieces and
salt and pepper. Heat
thoroughly. Top with chopped
parsley. Serve hot.

Kalakeitto

Finnish fish soup

4 servings

> 2 medium potatoes, peeled
> and cubed
> 2 cups water
> 1 teaspoon salt
> 1 pound frozen haddock fillets,
> cut into bite size pieces
> 3 tablespoons margarine or
> butter
> 2 tablespoons flour
> 2 cups milk
> Dash white pepper
> 2 tablespoons chopped fresh
> dill or parsley

Cook potatoes in salted water
about 10 minutes; add fish;
simmer 15 minutes. In the
meantime, melt margarine in
saucepan. Stir in flour; add milk
gradually, stirring constantly.
Add to soup and cook, stirring
constantly, for another 3
minutes. Top with chopped dill
or parsley.

Skånsk kålsoppa

Skansk cabbage soup

4 servings

1 small (about 1 pound)
*   smoked pork shoulder*
6 cups water
1 bay leaf
5 peppercorns
5 allspice berries
1 small head cabbage (about
*   1 pound), shredded*
2 medium carrots, sliced
4 medium potatoes, cut into
*   ½" cubes*
2 scallions, sliced
1 teaspoon salt
*   Dash pepper*
*   Chopped parsley*

In a saucepan, bring the water
to a boil, add the pork and
reduce heat. Skim off fat. Add
bay leaf, peppercorns and
allspice; simmer about 30
minutes. Add vegetables; cook
until tender. Remove pork and
cut into pieces. Return to soup.
Add pepper and salt. Sprinkle
with parsley before serving.

Grönkålssoppa

Swedish kale soup

4 servings

1 (10½-ounce) can cream of
*   chicken soup*
1 cup milk
2 cups boiling water
2 chicken bouillon cubes
1 (10-ounce) package frozen
*   chopped kale, thawed*
1 teaspoon salt
¼ teaspoon pepper
2 tablespoons chopped parsley
2 hard-cooked eggs

In a large saucepan, combine
soup, milk, and boiling water in
which bouillon cubes have been
dissolved. Add kale. Place
mixture in blender for a few
seconds on medium speed just
until kale is very finely chopped;
do not puree. Return to
saucepan; simmer 10 minutes.
Add salt and pepper. Garnish
with chopped parsley and
quartered hard-cooked eggs.

Kesäkeitto

Finnish summer soup

6 to 8 servings

2½ cups water
1 tablespoon sugar
¼ teaspoon salt
2½ cups milk
1 (10 ounce) package frozen
*   peas*
½ head cauliflower, cut into
*   flowerets*
1 medium carrot, diced
5 small potatoes, peeled and
*   quartered*
1 egg yolk
2 tablespoons margine or
*   butter*
1 tablespoon chopped chervil or
*   parsley*

In a large saucepan, bring water,
sugar, and salt to a boil. Add
milk, peas, cauliflower, carrot
and potatoes; simmer 10–15
minutes, or until vegetables are
tender. Stir 2–3 tablespoons of
hot soup into beaten egg yolk,
then return to soup. Season to
taste. Add margarine and chervil
or parsley. Serve immediately.

Blomkålspuré

Norwegian cauliflower puree

4 servings

1 large cauliflower
2 cups water
1 tablespoon margarine or
*   butter*
1½ tablespoons flour
4 chicken bouillon cubes
4 cups boiling water
½ teaspoon salt
¼ teaspoon white pepper
1 egg yolk, beaten
¼ cup heavy cream

Trim and wash cauliflower;
separate into flowerets. In a
large saucepan, cover cauliflower
with salted water, bring to a
boil and cook 10 minutes. Drain
and puree cauliflower in blender.
Melt margarine in small
saucepan; stir in flour until well
blended. Dissolve bouillon cubes
in boiling water; gradually stir
into margarine mixture. Cook,
stirring constantly, until slightly
thickened. Stir in pureed
cauliflower, salt and pepper.
In a small bowl, mix egg yolk
with heavy cream and 2 or 3
tablespoons of the hot soup.
Blend well, and stir into soup.
Serve hot.

Brunkaalsuppe

Danish brown cabbage soup

4 servings

½ *cup margarine or butter*
1 *small head cabbage, shredded*
1 *tablespoon sugar*
2 *(10½ ounce) cans beef consomme*
2 *cans water*
1 *teaspoon salt*
½ *teaspoon pepper*
1 *tablespoon chopped parsley*

In a large saucepan, melt margarine. Add cabbage; stir frequently, until cabbage is coated with margarine. Sprinkle with sugar; saute over low heat 3 minutes, stirring occasionally. Add consomme, water, salt and pepper. Cover; simmer over low heat about 20 minutes or until cabbage is tender. Sprinkle with parsley before serving.

Grönsakssoppa

Swedish vegetable soup

4 to 6 servings

1 *onion, chopped*
3 *carrots, sliced*
3 *tablespoons margarine or butter*
5 *cups hot water*
1 *beef bouillon cube*
3 *potatoes, peeled and diced*
2 *leeks or scallions, sliced*
½ *head cauliflower, divided into flowerets*
4 *stalks celery, chopped*
2 *teaspoons salt*
½ *teaspoon white pepper*

In a heavy saucepan, saute onion and carrots in margarine until onion is transparent. Add water, bouillon cube, potatoes, leeks, cauliflower, celery, salt, and pepper. Cover; cook over low heat 15 to 20 minutes or until vegetables are tender.

Hernekeitto

Finnish pea soup

6 servings

¾ *pound green split peas*
8 *cups water*
1 *ham hock or ham bone*
1 *carrot, chopped*
1 *medium onion, chopped*
2 *teaspoons salt*
½–1 *teaspoon pepper*

Soak peas in water about 12 hours. In a large pan, bring peas to boil in same water; skim. Add meat, carrot, and onion; simmer about 2 hours, or until peas are tender. Remove ham bone; return any pieces of ham to soup. Add salt and pepper.

Körvelsuppe

Danish chervil soup

4 servings

½ *pound young carrots, scraped*
4 *cups chicken bouillon*
3 *tablespoons margarine or butter*
3 *tablespoons flour*
4 *tablespoons chopped chervil*
½ *teaspoon salt*
¼ *teaspoon pepper*
Croutons

Cook whole carrots in bouillon for 10 to 15 minutes or until tender. Strain; reserve bouillon; puree carrots. In a heavy saucepan, melt margarine, stir in flour; gradually add bouillon, stirring constantly. Cook 5 minutes; add pureed carrots and chervil; stir well. Add salt and pepper. Sprinkle with croutons just before serving.

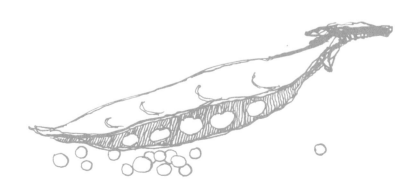

Aeblesuppe

Danish apple soup

4 servings

  5 *medium apples, unpeeled*
  4 *cups water*
½ *teaspoon grated lemon rind*
  2 *tablespoons cornstarch*
¼ *cup cold water*
½ *cup white wine*
½ *cup sugar*
  1 *teaspoon cinnamon*

Quarter apples, simmer in water with grated lemon rind for 5 minutes; strain. Add cornstarch which has been dissolved in cold water, stirring constantly. Add wine, sugar, and cinnamon; simmer 5 minutes. Serve hot or cold.

Ölsupa

Swedish bread soup

4 servings

  3 *tablespoons margarine or*
     butter
  1 *tablespoon flour*
  4 *cups beef bouillon*
1½ *cups dry pumpernickel*
     bread crumbs
  1 *tablespoon sugar*
  4 *small cooked sausages,*
     chopped
¼ *cup heavy cream*

In a heavy saucepan melt margarine; stir in flour. Gradually add hot bouillon, stirring constantly. Add pumpernickel bread crumbs and sugar. Cook over low heat about 30 minutes. Warm sausages in the soup during last 5 minutes of cooking. Stir in the cream; serve immediately.

Sauces

Ljus grundsås

Swedish sauce velouté

Makes 1 cup

- 2 tablespoons margarine or butter
- 2 tablespoons flour
- 1 chicken or beef bouillon cube
- 1 cup hot water

Melt margarine in small saucepan over medium heat. Stir in flour until well blended. Dissolve bouillon cube in water; gradually stir into flour mixture. Cook over medium heat, stirring constantly, until thickened and bubbly.

Skarp sovs

Danish sharp sauce

Makes 1½ cups

- 1 cup mayonnaise
- ½–1 teaspoon dry mustard
- 1 tablespoon lemon juice
- ½ cup heavy cream, whipped
- 1 tablespoon chopped dill or
- ½ teaspoon dill weed

Combine mayonnaise, mustard and lemon juice; blend well. Fold in whipped cream and dill. Serve with baked fish or vegetable salads.

Gravlaxsås

Swedish sauce for salmon

Makes ¾ cup

- 7 tablespoons oil
- 2 tablespoons vinegar
- 2 tablespoons prepared mustard
- 1 egg yolk
- 1 tablespoon sugar
- ¼ teaspoon salt
- ¼ teaspoon dill weed

Combine all ingredients in small jar; cover. Shake vigorously until well blended. Serve over pickled salmon or fish.

Pepparrotssås

Swedish horseradish sauce

Makes 1½ cups

- 1 recipe sauce velouté, page 30
- ½ cup heavy cream
- 2–3 tablespoons horseradish

Prepare sauce veloute according to directions. Stir in cream and horseradish. Serve with poached fish or boiled beef.

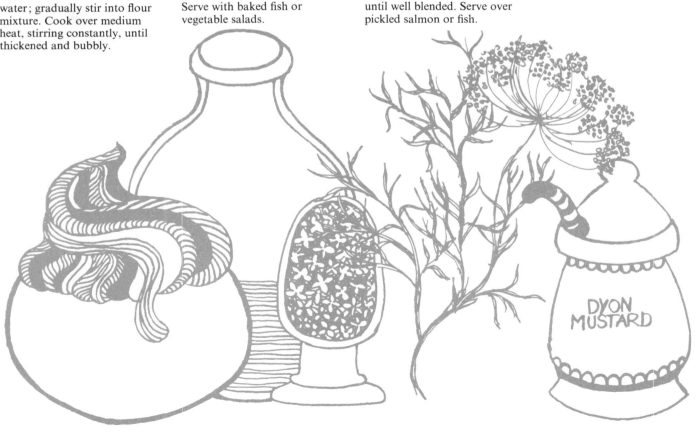

Skånsk senapssås

Skansk mustard sauce

Makes 1 cup

  1 cup sour cream
  1 tablespoon prepared mustard
  1 teaspoon instant minced
     onion
  1 teaspoon lemon juice
  ¼ teaspoon salt
  ⅛ teaspoon black pepper
  1 tablespoon chopped scallion

Combine all ingredients; blend well. Serve with fish or egg dishes.

Gräslökssås

Swedish chive sauce

Makes ¾ cup

  ½ cup margarine or butter
  3 egg yolks
  2 tablespoons lemon juice
  ¼ teaspoon salt
  1 tablespoon chopped chives

Heat margarine until bubbly but not brown. Place egg yolks, lemon juice, and salt in blender jar. Blend on low speed. Immediately pour in margarine in a slow stream. Add chives; beat 10 seconds. Serve with fish.

Äggsås

Swedish egg sauce

Makes 1¼ cups

  ¼ cup margarine or butter
  1 tablespoon flour
  1 cup milk
  2 teaspoons prepared mustard
  ½ teaspoon salt
     Dash black pepper
  2 hard cooked eggs, chopped
  2 teaspoons chopped parsley

Melt margarine in small saucepan over medium heat. Stir in flour until well blended. Gradually stir milk into flour mixture until well blended. Stir in mustard, salt and pepper. Cook over medium heat, stirring constantly until thickened and bubbly. Stir in eggs and parsley. Serve with fish.

Remouladesås

Remoulade sauce

Makes 1¼ cups

  ½ cup mayonnaise
  ½ cup sour cream
  5 gherkin pickles, chopped
  1 scallion, finely chopped
  1 tablespoon capers
  1 teaspoon chopped chives
  1 teaspoon chopped parsley
     Dash black pepper

Combine all ingredients; blend well. Serve with fish and shellfish.

Vegetables

Rödkaalssalat

Danish red cabbage salad

4 servings

- *1 cup finely shredded red cabbage*
- *2 medium apples, coarsely grated*
- *1 medium onion, chopped*
- *1 teaspoon caraway seed, crushed*
- *2 tablespoons French dressing*

Combine all ingredients; toss lightly.

Vitkåls-och apelsinsallad

Swedish cabbage and orange salad

4 servings

- *1 cup finely shredded white cabbage*
- *2 naval oranges, sectioned*
- *¼ cup raisins*
- *1 tablespoon salad oil*
- *1 tablespoon lemon juice*

Combine cabbage, oranges, and raisins. Add oil and lemon juice; toss well. Chill thoroughly. Serve with meat and fish dishes.

Vitkåls-och lingonsallad

Swedish cabbage and cranberry salad

4 servings

- *1 cup finely shredded cabbage*
- *¾ cup whole cranberry sauce*
- *1 tablespoon lemon juice*
- *¼ teaspoon salt*

Combine cabbage, cranberry sauce, lemon juice, and salt; toss lightly. Chill thoroughly.

Vitkåls-och äppelsallad

Swedish cabbage and apple salad

4 servings

- *2 cups shredded Savoy cabbage*
- *2 medium apples, sliced*
- *¼ cup orange juice*
- *¼ teaspoon salt*
- *1 tablespoon lemon juice*
- *½ cup cream, whipped*

Combine shredded cabbage, apple slices, orange juice, lemon juice, and salt; mix well. Carefully stir in whipped cream. Chill.

Morots- och äppelsallad

Swedish carrot and apple salad

4 servings

  2 *large carrots, grated*
  2 *medium apples, grated*
  1 *tablespoon lemon juice*

Combine carrots, apples, and lemon juice; toss lightly. Chill thoroughly. Serve with fish dishes.

Rödbedesalat

Danish beet salad

4 to 6 servings

  1 *(16 ounce) jar pickled beets, drained*
  2 *medium apples, thinly sliced*
  ½ *cup mayonnaise*

Combine sliced beets and apples; stir in mayonnaise. Chill well. Serve with cold meat or smoked fish.

Råkostkabarét

Norwegian raw vegetable medley

4 to 6 servings

  1 *cup finely shredded cabbage*
  2 *cooked beets, coarsely grated*
  2 *carrots, coarsely grated*
  1 *apple, peeled and grated*
  1 *tablespoon lemon juice*
  ½ *cup mayonnaise*
  2 *tablespoons milk*

Combine cabbage, beets, carrots, and grated apple; mix in lemon juice. Blend mayonnaise with milk; add to vegetables and toss to mix well. (If preferred, group vegetables separately and serve mayonnaise dressing in separate dish.)

Inkokta rödbetor

Swedish pickled beets

4 servings

  4 *pounds small beets (about 4 bunches)*
  2½ *cups boiling water*
  1 *cup vinegar*
  1½ *teaspoons salt*
  1 *cup sugar*
  10 *cloves*
  10 *peppercorns*
  2 *teaspoons horseradish*

Cook beets until tender; peel under running cold water. In a saucepan, mix hot water, vinegar, salt, sugar, cloves, peppercorns, and horseradish. Place cooked beets in a 3 quart casserole. Pour in hot pickling mixture. Cover with plastic wrap and cool. Refrigerate overnight.

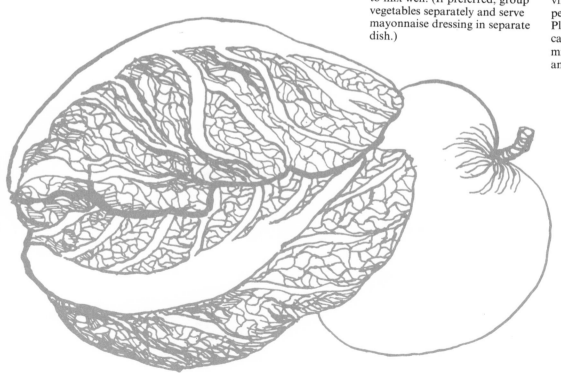

Syltede agurker

Danish pickled cucumbers

6 to 8 servings

     3 *medium cucumbers*
    ½ *cup vinegar*
    ½ *cup water*
     2 *tablespoons sugar*
     1 *teaspoon salt*
    ¼ *teaspoon ground white
        pepper
        Chopped parsley*

Peel cucumbers, if desired;
slice very thinly into serving
bowl. Combine remaining
ingredients; beat with fork.
Pour over cucumbers. Cover;
chill at least one hour before
serving. Sprinkle with chopped
parsley before serving.

Halländsk långkål

Halländsk kale

4 to 6 servings

     2 *(10 ounce) packages frozen
        chopped kale*
     2 *cups water*
    ½ *teaspoon salt*
    ½ *cup diced cooked salt pork*
     2 *tablespoons cornstarch*
    ½ *teaspoon ground ginger*
     1 *cup milk*
     2 *tablespoons maple syrup
        Dash ground white pepper
        Salt, if needed*

Place kale, water, salt and diced
pork in 2-quart saucepan.
Cover, bring to a boil; reduce
heat and simmer until kale is
tender, about 15 to 20 minutes.
Drain. Blend cornstarch and
ginger with milk; stir into kale
with syrup and pepper. Cook
over medium heat, stirring
constantly, until mixture has
thickened. Taste, add salt, if
needed.

Stekt lök

Norwegian fried onions

4 servings

     2 *tablespoons margarine or
        butter*
     4 *medium onions, peeled and
        thinly sliced*
     1 *teaspoon salt*
     1 *teaspoon Worcestershire
        sauce*
     1 *tablespoon chopped parsley*

In large frying pan, melt
margarine, add onions and salt;
saute over medium heat,
stirring occasionally, until
transparent and golden brown
Stir in Worcestershire sauce.
Sprinkle with parsley before
serving.

Rödkål

Braised cabbage

6 servings

     4 *tablespoons margarine or
        butter*
     2 *pounds white cabbage,
        shredded*
     1 *beef bouillon cube*
     1 *cup boiling water*
     2 *tablespoons maple or dark
        corn syrup*
    ⅓ *cup vinegar*
    ½ *teaspoon salt*

In a large heavy saucepan, melt
margarine. Lightly brown
cabbage over moderately high
heat, turning frequently, about
5 minutes. Dissolve bouillon
cube in water. Add to cabbage
with syrup, vinegar, and salt;
toss with fork to blend. Cover;
cook over medium heat about
45 minutes or until cabbage is
tender. Remove cover during
last 10 minutes to allow any
excess liquid to evaporate. Serve
with Christmas ham or cooked
pork sausages.

The Finns have learned to prepare their simple fare with great imagination. They can turn the unpretentious turnip into a delectable dish.

Stuvade grönsaker

Swedish creamed vegetables

6 to 8 servings

- ¼ cup water
- ½ teaspoon salt
- 1 (10 ounce) package frozen succotash
- 1 (10 ounce) package frozen peas and onions
- 1 (9 ounce) package frozen Italian green beans
- 4 tablespoons flour
- ½ teaspoon salt
- ¼ teaspoon ground white pepper
- 1½ cups milk
- 3 tablespoons margarine or butter
- 2 tablespoons chopped parsley

Bring water to a boil in 2-quart saucepan, add salt. Add succotash, cover and simmer for 7 minutes. Add peas and onions, cover, return to simmer and cook 4 minutes. Add beans, cover, return to simmer and cook 2 to 4 minutes or until all vegetables are tender. *Do not overcook.* Measure liquid and make up to one cup, adding water if necessary; add to vegetables. Stir flour, salt and pepper into cold milk; add to vegetables. Bring to a boil, stirring constantly; reduce heat and simmer until thickened, about 1 to 2 minutes. Stir in margarine. Sprinkle with parsley.

Kermaanmuhennetut porkkanat

Finnish creamed carrots

4 servings

- 2 tablespoons margarine or butter
- 3 tablespoons flour
- 1 tablespoon sugar
  Dash of ground white pepper
- 1 cup milk
- ½ cup half-and-half
- 1 (1 pound) can sliced carrots, drained
  Chopped parsley

Melt margarine; add flour, sugar and pepper. Stir until well-blended. Remove from heat, slowly add milk and half-and-half; return to heat. Simmer, stirring constantly, until thickened. Add drained carrots; heat. Garnish with chopped parsley.

Lanttulaatikko

Finnish turnip pie

6 servings

- 2 pounds yellow turnip, peeled and cut into ½" cubes
- ½ teaspoon salt
- 1½ cups fine dry bread crumbs
- 1 cup half-and-half
- 1 tablespoon sugar
  Dash ground white pepper
- ⅛ teaspoon ground nutmeg
- 2 eggs, lightly beaten
- 2 tablespoons margarine or butter

Cook turnip in just enough salted water to cover until tender, about 30 minutes. Drain and mash. Stir in 1 cup of the bread crumbs, half-and-half, sugar, pepper and nutmeg. Taste and add salt, if needed. Stir in beaten eggs. Use part of the margarine to grease a 9" round cake tin, about 2" deep. Coat with 1 to 2 tablespoons of remaining crumbs. Spread turnip mixture in pan, sprinkle with remaining crumbs and dot with remaining margarine. Bake in a slow oven (325°) 1 hour or until lightly browned.

Punajuuripihvit

Finnish beet steaks

4 servings

- 1 (1 pound) can sliced beets, drained
- 1 egg, lightly beaten
- ½ cup fine dry bread crumbs
- 2 tablespoons margarine or butter
- 1 tablespoon lemon juice
- 1 tablespoon chopped parsley

Dip beets in beaten egg. Sprinkle half of bread crumbs on paper towels; place beet slices on crumbs and sprinkle with remaining crumbs. Melt margarine in skillet. Sauté beet slices, turning to brown each side. Place on platter, sprinkle with lemon juice and parsley.

Lanttu

Finnish turnip

4 to 6 servings

> 2 tablespoons margarine or
>   butter
> 2 pounds yellow turnip, peeled
>   and cut into ½" cubes
> 2 teaspoons salt
> 2 beef bouillon cubes
> 2 cups boiling water
>   Parsley sprigs

Melt margarine in 2-quart
saucepan. Sauté turnip cubes
over medium heat, turning
occasionally to brown lightly on
all sides. Sprinkle with salt; add
bouillon cubes and water. Bring
to a boil; cover, reduce heat
and simmer until tender about
25 minutes. Garnish with
parsley.

Rotmos

Mashed Swedes

4 to 6 servings

> 1 pound yellow turnips, peeled
>   and cut into ½" cubes
> 2 beef bouillon cubes
> 2 cups boiling water
> ½ teaspoon salt
> ⅛ teaspoon ground white pepper
> ⅛ teaspoon ground allspice
> 1½ pounds potatoes, peeled and
>   cut into ½" cubes

Place turnip cubes into 2-quart
saucepan. Add bouillon cubes,
water, salt, pepper and allspice.
Boil about 15 minutes or until
half-cooked; add potatoe cubes;
cook 15 minutes more or until
tender. Drain and mash
vegetables; if needed, add a
little of the drained liquid.

Raggmunkar

Danish fried potato cakes

4 servings

> 1 egg
> 1 cup flour
> 2 cups milk
> 1½ teaspoons salt
> 6 medium potatoes, peeled,
>   cut into 1" cubes
> ¼ cup salad oil

In blender jar, combine egg,
flour, milk and salt; blend
½ minute. Add a few pieces of
potato at a time until all are
blended into batter. Heat a thin
layer of oil on a griddle or
frying pan; use about 1
tablespoon batter for small
cakes or 2 to 3 tablespoons for
large crepe-type cake, spreading
thinly. Fry on both sides until
crisp and brown. Serve with a
fruit preserve, maple syrup, or
plain with meat.

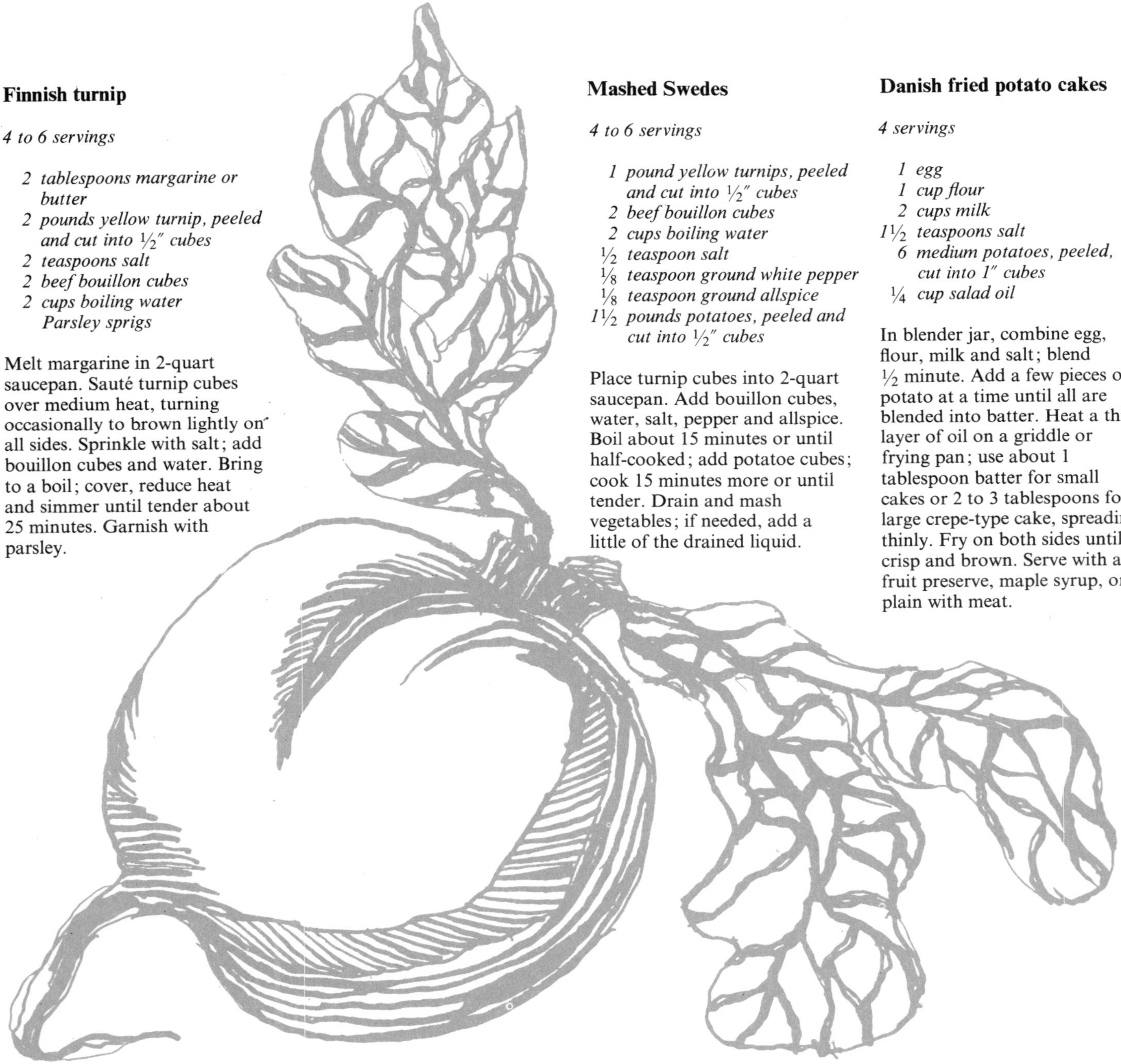

The turnip is a substantial and wholesome vegetable that goes well with a choice cut of pork.

Danish fried potato cakes

Potetboller

Norwegian potato balls

4 servings

    1 cup boiling water
    1 cup dry instant mashed
       potatoes
    8 canned anchovy fillets,
       finely minced
    1 tablespoon flour
    1 tablespoon chopped parsley
    ½ teaspoon salt
    ½ teaspoon dry mustard
    ¼ teaspoon pepper
    ⅛ teaspoon mace
    1 egg yolk
    1 cup bread crumbs
       Oil for deep frying

Add boiling water to instant
mashed potatoes. Add finely
minced anchovy fillets, flour,
parsley, salt, mustard, pepper
and mace; mix well. Form into
walnut-sized balls, coat with
beaten egg yolk, then bread
crumbs, and deep fry in hot oil
(375°) a few at a time until
golden brown.

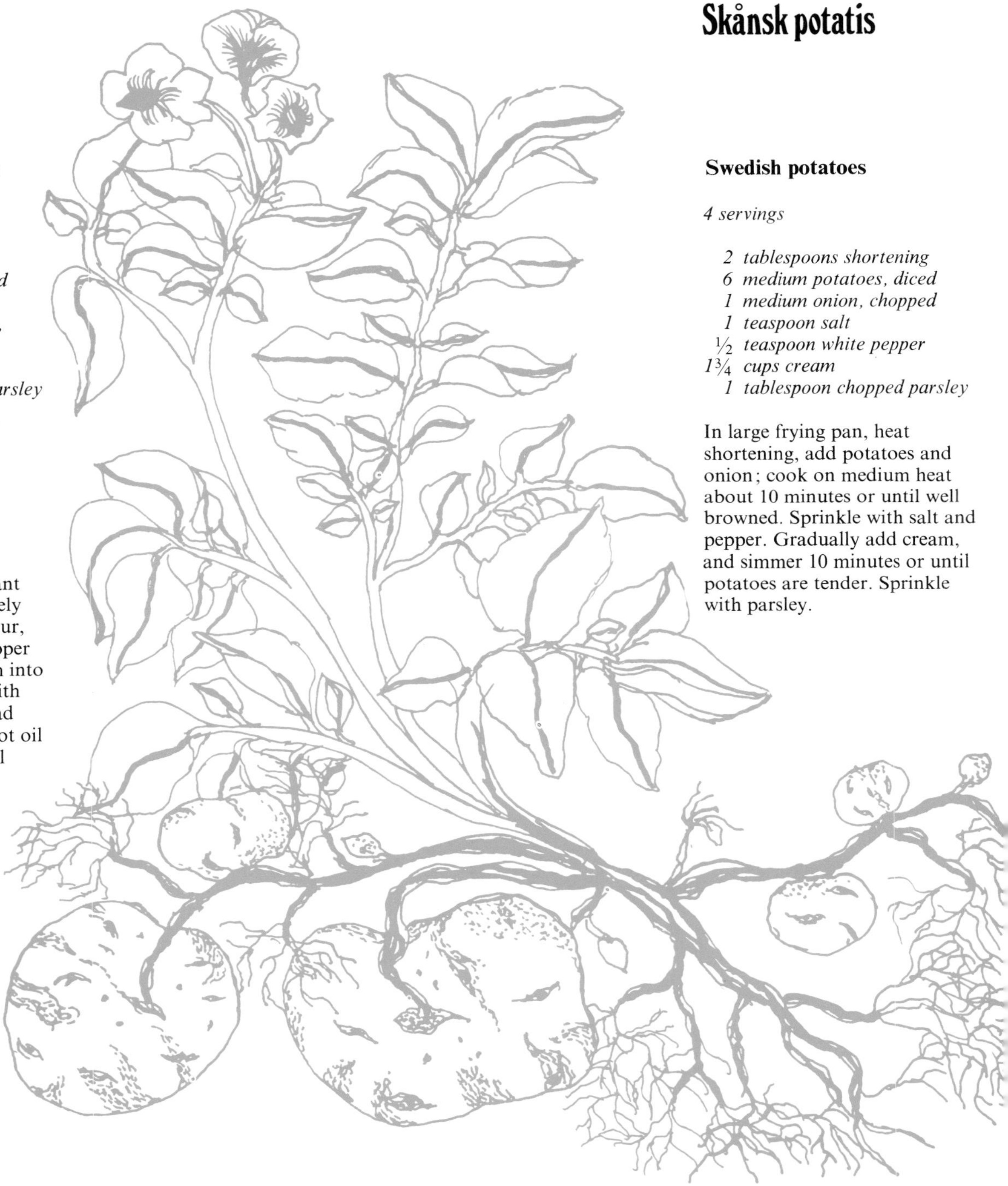

Skånsk potatis

Swedish potatoes

4 servings

    2 tablespoons shortening
    6 medium potatoes, diced
    1 medium onion, chopped
    1 teaspoon salt
    ½ teaspoon white pepper
  1¾ cups cream
    1 tablespoon chopped parsley

In large frying pan, heat
shortening, add potatoes and
onion; cook on medium heat
about 10 minutes or until well
browned. Sprinkle with salt and
pepper. Gradually add cream,
and simmer 10 minutes or until
potatoes are tender. Sprinkle
with parsley.

In Scandinavia a potato is not simply a potato – it is a chance to experiment and improvise. Since it is part of the staple diet in the Nordic countries, a wide range of varieties is always available, and it is possible to be served a different potato dish every day for weeks.

Brunede kartofler

Danish browned potatoes

4 servings

> 2 pounds small potatoes, unpeeled
> ½ cup sugar
> 3 tablespoons margarine or butter

Boil potatoes in their skins; peel while still hot. In a saucepan, brown the sugar and add margarine, stirring constantly. Add potatoes and turn carefully until potatoes are coated on all sides.

Stuvad potatis

Swedish style creamed potatoes

4 servings

> 1½ tablespoons margarine or butter
> 1½ tablespoons flour
> 1¾ cups light cream
> 6 medium boiled potatoes, sliced or diced
> 1 teaspoon salt
> ½ teaspoon white pepper
> 1 tablespoon chopped dill, chives or parsley

In a saucepan, heat margarine, stir in flour; add cream; cook 5 minutes over moderate heat. Stir constantly. Add potatoes, salt and pepper; heat thoroughly. Garnish with chopped herb.

Muhennetut perunat

Finnish stewed potatoes

4 servings

> 6 medium potatoes, sliced or diced
> 2 cups light cream
> 1 teaspoon salt
> ½ teaspoon white pepper
> 1 tablespoon finely-chopped chives

Place potatoes in a heavy saucepan; add 1½ cups cream; bring to a boil; reduce heat and simmer over very low heat. Gradually add remaining cream, (just enough to be absorbed by time the potatoes are tender). Season with salt and pepper. Sprinkle with chopped chives.

Imullytetty perunalaatikko

Finnish sweetened potato pudding

4 servings

> 6 medium boiled potatoes, hot
> 4 tablespoons flour
> 2 tablespoons sugar
> 1 tablespoon salt
> 3 cups milk
> 4 tablespoons margarine or butter

Slice potatoes and place into buttered 2-quart mold. Sprinkle mixture of flour and sugar over each layer. Add salt, milk and margarine. Bake in a moderate oven (350°) for 40 minutes or until golden brown.

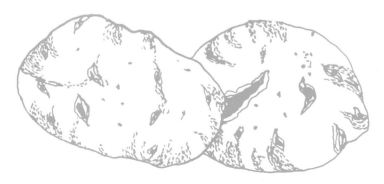

Småländska raggmunkar

Smalandsk potato cakes

4 servings

2½ pounds potatoes, peeled, and
     cut into large cubes
1½ teaspoons salt
     Water, if needed
½ cup oil

Start blender on high speed.
Add potato cubes a few at a
time until finely chopped. Add
salt, and if mixture is very thick,
add a drop or two of water.
Heat large, heavy skillet; cover
surface with thin layer of oil.
For each cake, pour 2 to 3
tablespoons of potato mixture
onto hot pan; spread thinly.
Brown well on each side over
moderate heat until cakes are
very crisp. Drain on paper
towels. Serve immediately.

Hasselbackspotatis

Finnish hasselback potatoes

4 servings

12 oval-shaped potatoes, peeled
 1 teaspoon salt
 3 tablespoons margarine or
     butter
 4 tablespoons grated Parmesan
     cheese
 2 tablespoons bread crumbs

Cut potatoes into thin slices,
but not quite through to the
lower edge, so that the slices
hold together. Place potatoes,
with slices upward, into a
well-buttered casserole. Sprinkle
with salt and dot with bits of
margarine. Bake in a very
hot oven (450°) 20 minutes;
basting occasionally. Sprinkle
with cheese and bread crumbs
and bake another 25 minutes
without basting.

Indkogt fisk

Danish poached fish

4 servings

  1 *quart water*
  2 *teaspoons salt*
  2 *tablespoons vinegar*
  3 *peppercorns*
  5 *whole allspice*
  1 *bay leaf*
  2 *pounds whole, cleaned fish*
    or fish fillets (cod, haddock,
    mackerel)
    Dill or parsley

In a large saucepan, combine water, salt, vinegar, peppercorns, allspice, and bay leaf. Bring to a boil and boil for 10 to 15 minutes. Add fish. Cover; simmer 6 to 8 minutes. Remove from heat; allow fish to cool in bouillon. Remove fish from bouillon and garnish with dill or parsley.

Fiskepudding

Norwegian fish mold

4 to 6 servings

  2 *(1 pound) packages frozen
     haddock fillets, thawed*
  2 *teaspoons salt*
  ¼ *teaspoon black pepper*
  1 *cup milk*
  1 *cup cream or evaporated
     milk*
1½ *tablespoons cornstarch*
  1 *tablespoon margarine or
     butter*
  4 *tablespoons dry bread crumbs*

In blender, add fish fillets, salt,
pepper, milk, and cream in
small amounts; blend until
mixture is thoroughly pureed.
Beat in cornstarch. Butter a
2-quart mold; sprinkle with
bread crumbs until completely
covered; remove excess crumbs.
Carefully pour in pureed fish
mixture. Place mold in pan of
hot water. Bake in a moderate
oven (350°) about 1 hour or until
top of mold is firm to touch.
Unmold carefully on platter and
serve warm.

Fiskeboller

Norwegian fish balls

4 to 6 servings

  1 *(1 pound) package frozen
     cod fillets, thawed*
  1 *teaspoon salt*
  ⅔ *cup heavy cream or
     evaporated milk*
  2 *eggs*
  1 *tablespoon cornstarch*
  1 *quart water*
  2 *bouillon cubes*

Cut fish into pieces. Place half
of the fish in blender jar.
Combine cream, eggs, and
cornstarch. Pour half of cream
mixture into blender jar. Blend
thoroughly. Empty into small
mixing bowl. Repeat with
remaining fish and cream
mixture. Stir all the blended fish
mixture together. Chill
thoroughly. Pour water into a
large, wide saucepan. Add
bouillon cubes; bring to a boil.
Lower heat so that bouillon is
just simmering. Using two
teaspoons to make balls, drop
fish mixture into bouillon. Cook
for 8 to 10 minutes. Remove
balls with slotted spoon and
keep warm. Serve with
horseradish sauce.

Kogt torskerogn

Danish cod roe

4 servings

1¾ *pounds cod roe*
  2 *quarts water*
  2 *tablespoons salt*
  2 *tablespoons chopped dill or
     parsley*

Carefully wash roe; do not break
membrane. In a large 3-quart
saucepan, heat water with salt
and dill to boiling. Reduce heat
and bring water to a simmer.
Gently put in roe. Simmer until
done about 5 to 10 minutes
depending on size. Carefully
remove roe and serve with lemon
slices.

Kokt torsk

Norwegian cod

4 servings

1½ *quarts water*
  3 *tablespoons salt*
  4 *cod steaks, ¾" thick*
  ¼ *pound margarine or butter,
     melted*
  1 *tablespoon chopped parsley*
  1 *tablespoon chopped chives*
  ½ *teaspoon salt*
  ⅛ *teaspoon black pepper*

In a large saucepan, bring water
and salt to a boil. Carefully add
fish steaks. Reduce heat so that
water just simmers; cook 5 to 8
minutes. Remove fish from
water with slotted spoon; keep
warm. Stir together melted
margarine, parsley, chives, salt
and pepper. Heat mixture to the
simmering point. Serve sauce
with cod steaks.

Gryderet med torsk

Danish cod fish casserole

4 servings

1 (1 pound) package frozen
 cod fillets, thawed
1 (2 ounce) can flat anchovies
3 tablespoons bread crumbs
3 tablespoons margarine or
 butter

Separate cod fillets. Drain
anchovies and chop finely;
spread over each fillet. Roll
fillets. Place in a buttered 1½
quart casserole, sprinkle on
bread crumbs; dot with
margarine. Bake in a moderate
oven (350°) 25 to 30 minutes or
until fish flakes when tested with
a fork.

Ovnsstekt fiskefilet

Norwegian baked fish fillets

3 to 4 servings

1 (1 pound) package frozen
 fish fillets (haddock or cod)
1 tablespoon lemon juice
1 egg, slightly beaten
¼ cup bread crumbs
2 tablespoons margarine or
 butter
1 lemon, sliced

Thaw fish fillets; place in
well-buttered 7″ × 11″ × 2″
baking dish. Sprinkle with
lemon juice; pour beaten egg
over fillets. Top with bread
crumbs and bits of margarine.
Bake in moderate oven (350°)
about 30 to 40 minutes or until
fish flakes when tested with a
fork. Garnish with lemon slices.

Rödspaette og spinat

Danish fried flounder with onion sauce

4 servings

1 (1 pound) package frozen
 flounder fillets, thawed
4 tablespoons flour
2 eggs, beaten
½ cup bread crumbs
4 tablespoons margarine or
 butter, melted
3 tablespoons margarine or
 butter

Onion sauce:

2 medium onions, finely
 chopped
2 tablespoons flour
½ teaspoon salt
¼ teaspoon black pepper
½ teaspoon sugar
1½ cups milk

Dip fillets in flour, then beaten
egg, and finally in bread crumbs.
Fry in large skillet in melted
margarine until golden brown.
Remove from skillet and keep
warm. Melt margarine and sauté
onions until transparent;
remove from skillet. Stir flour,
salt, pepper, and sugar into
remaining margarine in skillet;
gradually add milk. Cook and
stir until sauce thickens. Add
onions and cook, stirring
constantly, for 2 to 3 minutes.
Serve sauce with fried flounder
fillets, or Swedish fried herring
(recipe page 44).

Rödspaette med lögsovs

Danish flounder and spinach casserole

4 servings

1 (1 pound) package frozen
 flounder fillets, thawed
2 tablespoons flour
½ teaspoon salt
⅛ teaspoon black pepper
2 eggs, beaten
½ cup dry bread crumbs
¼ cup margarine or butter
1 (9 ounce) package frozen
 creamed spinach
1 (3 ounce) can sliced
 mushrooms

Separate fish fillets. Dust with
flour; sprinkle with salt and
pepper. Dip floured fillets in
beaten egg, then in bread
crumbs. Brown fillets in
margarine. Cook spinach
according to package directions.
Pour spinach in bottom of
shallow casserole. Top with
fillets and then mushrooms. Heat
in a moderate oven (350°) 15 to
20 minutes or until heated
thoroughly.

Not every fresh herring is soaked and pickled in a careful blend of savory sauces. Some still find their way into the frying pan, to come out a crisp golden brown.

(For recipe, see Swedish fried herring.)

Tasty Swedish herring balls

Stekt färsk sill

Swedish fried herring

4 servings

  2 pounds small herrings or
     smelts
  2 teaspoons salt
  4 tablespoons rye flour or dry
     bread crumbs
  3 tablespoons margarine or
     butter
  1 recipe onion sauce, page 43

Clean fish; remove backbones. Wash thoroughly and drain. Add salt to the rye flour or bread crumbs. Roll fish in flour or bread crumbs until well coated. Melt margarine in a large skillet and fry the fish about 3 to 4 minutes on each side. Serve with onion sauce (recipe page 43, 3rd column).

Sillbullar

Swedish herring balls

4 to 6 servings

  1 ($3\frac{1}{4}$ ounce) can kippered
     herring, drained
  4 cold boiled potatoes,
     mashed
  $\frac{1}{2}$ pound ground beef, cooked
     and drained
  1 small onion, chopped
  1 tablespoon flour
  $\frac{1}{2}$ teaspoon salt
  $\frac{1}{8}$ teaspoon black pepper
  2 tablespoons milk
  4 tablespoons dry bread
     crumbs
  3 tablespoons margarine or
     butter

Chop herring. Combine with potatoes, beef, and onion until well blended. Add flour, salt, and pepper. Stir in milk gradually, using a little more, if necessary, until mixture is of a consistency that can be shaped into 1″ balls. Roll balls in bread crumbs. Melt margarine in large heavy skillet; brown balls in margarine. Serve hot.

Swedish herring a l'Opera Cellar.
Fried seafood finds its perfect
accompaniment in ice-cold beer
and thinly sliced dark rye bread.

45

Strömming à la Opris

Swedish herring a l'Opera Cellar

4 servings

2 pounds frozen smelts, thawed
2 egg yolks
1 cup evaporated milk
⅓ cup rye flour
2 teaspoons salt
3 tablespoons margarine or
  butter

Clean smelts; remove backbones.
Blend egg yolks and milk. Add
smelts and let stand for a
half-hour. Carefully remove
smelts so that as much of the
milk as possible remains on fish.
Quickly dip in flour mixed with
salt, turning until coated. Melt
margarine in large skillet. Fry
smelts until medium brown,
about 3 to 4 minutes on each
side.

Fiskegryte

Norwegian tuna fish casserole

4 servings

- *1 (13 ounce) can tuna fish, drained*
- *1 (1 pound) package frozen cottage potato fries, thawed*
- *1 (15 ounce) can tomato sauce*
- *1 (3½ ounce) can french fried onions*
- *1 teaspoon Worcestershire sauce*
- *1 tablespoon chopped parsley*

Flake tuna fish. Arrange alternate layers of tuna fish, potatoes, tomato sauce and onions in a buttered 7″ × 11″ × 2″ baking dish. Sprinkle each tomato sauce layer with Worcestershire sauce and parsley. (Top layer should be onions.) Bake in a moderate oven (350°) 30 to 35 minutes or until tomato sauce bubbles.

Strömmingsflundror

Swedish fried flounder fillets

4 servings

- *1 (1 pound) package frozen flounder fillets, thawed*
- *4 tablespoons dry bread crumbs*
- *2 medium onions, thinly sliced*
- *3 tablespoons margarine or butter, melted*
- *½ cup cream*

Coat fish fillets with breadcrumbs. In a large skillet, sauté onions in melted margarine until transparent and golden brown. Remove onions from pan; keep warm. In the same skillet, fry fillets over moderate heat until golden brown, about 4 minutes on each side. Place fillets on platter; cover with cooked onions. Pour cream into skillet and heat almost to boil. Pour over fish fillets and onions. Serve immediately.

Fylld sild

Norwegian stuffed herring

4 servings

- *2 pounds fresh herring, smelts, or other small fish*
- *2 teaspoons salt*
- *2 tablespoons chopped chives*
- *2 tablespoons finely chopped onions*
- *¼ cup dry bread crumbs*
- *3 tablespoons margarine or butter*

Clean fish; remove backbones. Sprinkle with salt. Sandwich chives and onions between two fish; coat the fish sandwiches with bread crumbs. Melt margarine in a large skillet; fry fish until golden brown on both sides.

Janssons frestelse

Jansson's temptation

4 to 6 servings

- *3 medium onions, cut in rings*
- *2 tablespoons margarine or butter, melted*
- *6 potatoes, peeled and cut into ½″ strips*
- *1 (2 ounce) can anchovy fillets*
- *1 cup heavy cream or evaporated milk*

Sauté onion rings in margarine until golden brown. In a buttered 2-quart casserole, place alternate layers of potatoes, onion rings, and anchovies ending with a layer of potatoes. Carefully pour cream over top of potatoes; dot with margarine. Bake in moderate oven (350°) 45 to 50 minutes or until potatoes are tender.

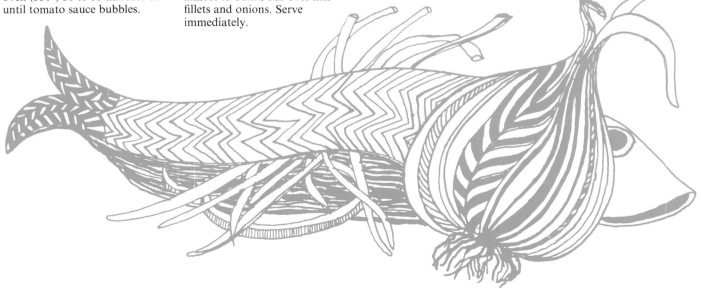

Ovnstegt fyldt fisk

Danish baked stuffed fish

4 servings

1 medium bluefish or mackerel
½ teaspoon salt
¼ teaspoon black pepper
2 tablespoons lemon juice
1 small onion, finely chopped
2 tablespoons margarine or
    butter
⅓ cup water
1 cup packaged bread stuffing

Clean fish; wash and dry.
Sprinkle with salt, pepper, and
lemon juice. Sauté onion in
margarine until transparent and
golden brown. Add onions and
water to stuffing mix. Fill cavity
with stuffing. Fasten edges with
wooden toothpicks. Place in
buttered baking dish. Bake in
moderately hot oven (375°)
35 to 40 minutes or until fish
flakes when tested with a fork.

Rökt fisk i folie

Danish fish in foil

6 servings

2 (1 pound) packages frozen
    fish fillets, thawed
1 teaspoon salt
¼ teaspoon black pepper
2 tablespoons lemon juice
1 (10½ ounce) can cream of
    shrimp soup
¼ cup cream or evaporated
    milk
1½ cups cooked shrimp, deveined

Arrange fillets on six pieces of
buttered aluminum foil about
12 inches square. Sprinkle with
salt, pepper, and lemon juice.
Combine soup, cream, and
shrimp. Spoon stuffing on half
of fish fillets; fold the other half
over stuffing. Fold foil over
stuffed fillets and fold edges
together to make a pocket.
Place in a large shallow baking
dish. Bake in a moderately hot
oven (375°) 25 to 30 minutes or
until fish flakes when tested with
a fork.

Sotare

Swedish chimney sweeps

4 servings

2 pounds fresh trout
2 tablespoons salad oil
2 teaspoons salt

Clean, rinse, and dry fish. Brush
with oil and sprinkle with salt.
Shape a shallow pan out of
several sheets of aluminum foil.
Brush pan with oil and place fish
in it. Place over glowing
charcoals and cook until fish
flakes easily when tested with a
fork. (Fish may be broiled in
broiler 4 to 5 minutes or until
done.)

Kräftor

Swedish crayfish

4 servings

6 quarts cold water
6 tablespoons salt
1 tablespoon dill seed
3 bunches fresh dill
40 crayfish or 4 lobsters

In a very large kettle bring
water, salt, dill seed, and 1 bunch
fresh dill to the boil. Drop
crayfish, 8 to 10 at a time, into
boiling water. Cook 6 to 7
minutes. (Or plunge lobsters into
boiling water; cook 10 minutes
for 2-pound lobsters, 7 minutes
for lobsters less than 2 pounds.)
Add fresh dill with each addition
of crayfish. Remove crayfish
from water; drain. Garnish with
remaining dill. Serve with
toast and melted butter, if
desired.

No buffet supper in Sweden is complete without shiny, chilled eel in aspic (left), pickled herring (right) and Jansson's temptation (below), recipe page 46, 4th column.

Seafood is an important ingredient in many Scandinavian dishes.

Glasmästarsill

Swedish pickled herring

4 servings

    2 salted schmalz herring,
      filleted and skinned
½ cup vinegar
    1 cup water
    1 small red or sweet white
      onion, thinly sliced
    4 bay leaves
    1 tablespoon black pepper
¾ cup sugar

Cover herring fillets with cold water; soak overnight in refrigerator. Drain and rinse; Cut into 1½″ pieces. Place in a non-metallic bowl. Combine remaining ingredients and pour over herring. Refrigerate at least 4 hours before serving. (Will keep for several days.)

Ålaladåb

Swedish eel in aspic

4 to 6 servings

1½ pounds eel or small trout
    1 (12 ounce) package frozen
      cleaned shrimp
      Water
    1 teaspoon salt
    1 medium onion, sliced
    4 peppercorns
    2 bay leaves
    2 tablespoons vinegar
    1 envelope unflavored gelatin
½ cup cold water
    2 hard cooked eggs, cut into
      wedges
    1 (10 ounce) package frozen
      tiny peas, cooked and cooled
      Parsley or dill

Skin and fillet eel or trout. Place in saucepan with shrimp; add water to cover. Add salt, onion, peppercorns and bay leaves. Heat until just below boiling; poach fish and shrimp until just tender, about 3 to 5 minutes. *Do Not Overcook.* Carefully remove fish and shrimp; strain liquid, stir in vinegar and reserve. Soften gelatin in cold water; stir into hot fish liquid until dissolved. Arrange shrimp in bottom of rinsed 1½-quart ring mold. Cover with gelatin-fish liquid. Arrange fish pieces and hard cooked egg wedges over shrimp, cover with more gelatin mixture. Arrange peas over fish pieces; cover with remaining gelatin mixture. Chill until set about 2 hours. Turn out on round platter. Serve cold, garnished with parsley or dill.

Fresh trout from icy Swedish mountain streams is first fried, and then marinated in vinegar with herbs.

Swedish smoked fish in foil

Stuvad fisk

Swedish sauced trout

4 servings

    1 recipe broiled trout, page 47
1½ cups vinegar
    ½ cup sugar
20 allspice berries
    3 bay leaves
    1 small white or red onion,
         thinly sliced
         Dill or parsley sprigs

Heat vinegar, sugar, allspice, bay leaves and sliced onion to boiling point. Remove from heat and leave to cool. Prepare trout according to directions for Swedish chimney sweeps (page 47, 3rd column). Place the fish in a bowl while still hot. Pour vinegar mixture over hot fish.

Fiskfilé i folie

Swedish smoked fish in foil

4 servings

    4 (½ pound each) smoked fish
    4 pieces foil, approximately
         12" square
    4 teaspoons water

Score skin of fish. Place one fish on each square of foil; sprinkle each with one teaspoon water. Bend edges of foil up to make a close-fitting pan, without covering top of fish. Place on cookie sheet. Bake in a very hot oven (450°) about 3 to 5 minutes, or until heated through. (The fish should be restored to a "just smoked" flavor, not browned or baked.)

Meat dishes

Denmark is a paradise for the lean and streamlined Danish hog. It is said that in this friendly, tidy land there are twice as many hogs as people. The Danes are naturally fond of their pork, but its fame has spread far beyond Denmark's borders. The English especially love delicious Danish pork chops, ham and Danish bacon, and consequently the Danes often find less of their own pork in stores than they would like, since most of it is exported. Meat is scarcer than fish throughout most of Scandinavia. And this is nowhere truer than in the remote mountains of Norway, where there is no land suitable for grazing cattle and beef has become a luxury item.

It is partly because of the need to be economical with meat that the Scandinavians are so good at making meatballs. Meatballs are nowhere more delicious than in these northern countries: delicate, soft and tender, carefully seasoned so that the flavor of the meat can be tasted in its own right when it is fried, and served with an exquisite cream sauce. No Swedish or Finnish smörgåsbord is complete without a pot of full-flavored brown meatballs accompanied by crisp cabbage.

Köttfärs

Swedish frosted meat loaf

4 to 6 servings

    1 recipe meat mixture page 50
    2 cups mashed potatoes
      Beef stock or hot water
    2 tablespoons cold water
    1 tablespoon cornstarch

Press meat mixture into a greased 9″ × 5″ × 3″ loaf pan. Bake in moderate oven (350°) for 1 hour. Pour off any cooking juices; measure and save. Let loaf cool in pan about 15 minutes. Turn loaf out of pan onto oven-proof platter or pan. Frost completely with mashed potatoes. Place in hot oven (450°) until edges of potatoes are golden brown, about 10 to 15 minutes. Measure reserved juices and add beef stock or water to make 1 cup. Blend cornstarch and water; add to juices. Cook over moderate heat, stirring constantly, until gravy comes to a boil. Taste; season with salt and pepper, if needed.

Köttbullar

Swedish meat balls

4 servings

Meat mixture:
    1 pound ground beef
    ¼ pound ground pork
    ½ cup fine dry bread crumbs
    1 cup milk
    ½ teaspoon salt
    ¼ teaspoon white pepper
    1 egg
    2 tablespoons finely chopped onion

Gravy:
    2 tablespoons margarine or butter
    1 cup half-and-half or beef stock
    1 tablespoon cornstarch
    2 tablespoons cold water

Combine meat mixture ingredients; beat with fork. Shape mixture into 8 large or 40 to 50 small meat balls. Heat margarine in large skillet over moderate heat. Brown meat balls on one side about 2 minutes; turn and brown other side. Reduce heat to low and cover pan; simmer about 15 minutes for large meat balls, 8 minutes for small. Remove meat balls; pour off fat. Add half-and-half or beef stock. Blend cornstarch and water; add to pan. Stir over moderate heat until mixture comes to a boil; taste and if necessary, add salt and pepper. Serve gravy with meat balls.

Frikadeller

Swedish meat dumplings

4 servings

    2 tablespoons fine dry bread crumbs
    ½ cup half-and-half
    ½ pound ground veal
    ½ pound ground pork
    2 egg yolks
    ½ teaspoon salt
      Dash ground white pepper
    4 bouillon cubes
    4 cups boiling water

Soak bread crumbs in half-and-half. Combine veal, pork, crumb mixture, egg yolks, salt and pepper; beat with fork. Using teaspoons, shape into small meat balls. In large saucepan, dissolve bouillon cubes into boiling water; add meat balls a few at a time. Simmer over moderate heat about 5 minutes. Remove with slotted spoon. Drain on paper towels; keep warm. Serve with a dill, lemon, tomato or caper sauce if desired.

Pannbiff

Swedish meat cakes garni

4 servings

- 1 pound ground beef
- 2 tablespoons margarine or butter
- ½ teaspoon salt
  Dash ground white pepper
- 4 large hamburger buns, toasted
- 4 tablespoons mayonnaise
- 4 tablespoons catsup
- 16 slices dill pickle
- 16 very thin slices tomato
- 4 slices sweet Bermuda onion
- 4 leaves lettuce
  Radish roses or parsley sprigs, if desired

Shape beef into four large round patties. In large skillet, melt margarine and cook patties over moderate heat until browned on both sides and center is cooked to desired degree of doneness. Sprinkle with salt and pepper. Spread each bun with 1 tablespoon mayonnaise, place patty on bun; spread 1 tablespoon catsup on each patty. Top each patty with 4 slices dill pickle, 4 slices tomato, 1 slice Bermuda onion and 1 lettuce leaf. Serve garnished with radish roses and parsley sprigs, if desired.

Kålpudding

Cabbage pudding

4 servings

- 1 (1½ pound) head cabbage
- ½ pound ground beef
- ½ pound ground pork
- 1 tablespoon margarine or butter
- ½ teaspoon salt
- ⅛ teaspoon black pepper
- 1 cup mashed potatoes

Remove core and chop cabbage into large pieces. Cook cabbage in boiling salted water only until cabbage wilts. Drain. Cook beef and pork in melted margarine. Combine cooked meat, salt, pepper, and potatoes. Arrange alternate layers of cabbage and meat and potato mixture in a 2-quart casserole. Cover. Bake in a moderate oven (350°) 45 to 50 minutes.

Kalvtimbal

Swedish veal timbale

6 servings

- 1 cup half-and-half
- 2 eggs, separated
- 2 tablespoons flour
- ¾ pound ground veal
- 3 tablespoons softened margarine or butter
- 1 teaspoon salt
- ¼ teaspoon ground white pepper
- 3 tablespoons fine dry bread crumbs

Combine half-and-half and egg yolks; stir in flour. Add mixture to veal with 2 tablespoons of the margarine, salt and pepper; beat well with fork. Beat egg whites until stiff; fold into meat mixture. Use remaining margarine to grease a 1½-quart casserole; sprinkle with bread crumbs, coating bottom and sides. Shake off excess; reserve. Turn meat mixture into casserole; sprinkle with reserved crumbs. Cover with lid or aluminum foil. Place in large baking pan filled to a depth of 1″ with boiling water. Bake in hot oven (400°) for 1 hour or until knife inserted near center comes out clean. Let stand 5 minutes; turn out onto warm serving platter.

Korvgryta

Swedish sausage casserole

4 servings

- 1 pound sausage meat
- 2 medium onions, sliced
- 2 apples, sliced
- 4–5 medium potatoes, cooked and sliced

Make 8 patties of sausage meat. Cook in a heavy skillet until lightly browned. Remove and keep warm. Pour off all but 2 tablespoons of drippings. Cook onions in drippings until golden brown and transparent. Add apple slices; cook until tender. In a 2-quart buttered casserole, arrange layers of potatoes, sausage and onion-apple mixture. Bake in a moderate oven (350°) 30 to 35 minutes, or until thoroughly heated.

Ham and asparagus, a classic combination of delicate flavors, with sweet cream, a characteristic Swedish touch.

Fyllda skinkrulader

Swedish ham rolls

4 servings

- 1 cup cooked green peas
- 1 apple, diced
- 1 teaspoon lemon juice
- 2 hard cooked eggs, chopped
- 1 teaspoon capers, chopped
- ½ cup heavy cream, whipped
- ½ cup mayonnaise
- 1 tablespoon grated horseradish
- 1 (10 ounce) package frozen asparagus spears, cooked and chilled
- 12 slices boiled ham, about ¾ pound

Combine peas, apple, lemon juice, eggs and capers; chill. In another bowl, blend cream, mayonnaise, and horseradish; chill. Stir ½ cup of the cream dressing into the peas and apple mixture. Place about ¼ cup of the mixture on half of the ham slices and roll to form logs. Place asparagus on remaining ham slices and roll into logs. Serve ham rolls with remaining dressing. Garnish with strips of pimento, if desired.

Leverböf

Danish ground liver steak

4 to 6 servings

- ¾ pound beef liver, cut into pieces
- 5 medium potatoes, peeled and cubed
- 1 teaspoon salt
- ¼ teaspoon black pepper
- 3 tablespoons margarine or butter
- 2 medium onions, thinly sliced
- 1 cup heavy cream

Using grinder or blender, finely chop liver and potatoes together. Add salt and pepper; mix well. Melt margarine in large skillet. Spoon liver-potato mixture into skillet to make 4 to 6 "steaks". Brown on one side about 3 minutes. Place a slice of onion on each "steak". Turn and brown on onion side for 2 to 3 minutes. Carefully remove "steaks" and keep warm. Pour cream into pan and heat to simmering point, stirring to blend with pan juices. Serve with liver "steaks".

A typical example of Danish resource-fulness – transforming ground liver into 'steaks,' and a delicacy even without the usual cream sauce.

Norwegian-style steak and onions

Biff med lök

Norwegian steak and onions

4 servings

- 2 medium onions, sliced
- 2 tablespoons margarine or butter
- 1½ pounds round steak, cut into ½″ slices
- 1 teaspoon salt
- ¼ teaspoon black pepper

In a large, heavy skillet, cook onions in margarine until lightly browned. Remove from pan and keep warm. Brown steak slices on each side about 3 minutes, adding additional margarine if necessary. Sprinkle with salt and pepper. Remove steak to serving dish; top with onions. Pour pan juices over steak and onions.

Biff à la Lindström

Swedish beef a la Lindstrom

4 servings

 1 pound ground beef
 1 cup mashed potatoes
 1 egg
 1 teaspoon salt
 ¼ teaspoon pepper
 ½ cup chopped pickled beets
 2 tablespoons finely chopped
   onion
 2 tablespoons capers, chopped
 3 tablespoons margarine or
   butter

Mix together ground beef, mashed potatoes, egg, salt, pepper, beets, onion, and capers. Shape into eight patties. Melt margarine in a large skillet; brown patties on each side for 4 to 5 minutes.

Pepparrotskött

Swedish boiled beef

4 servings

 2½–3 pounds beef chuck with
   bone
 1 quart water
 2 teaspoons salt
 1 onion, peeled and quartered
 2 carrots, cut into 1″ slices
 1 small yellow turnip, diced
 2 stalks celery, cut into 1″
   slices
 1 tablespoon margarine or
   butter
 2 tablespoons flour
 1 bouillon cube
 1 cup milk
 2–3 teaspoons grated
   horseradish

Place meat in large, heavy saucepan; cover with water. Add salt and onion. Bring to a boil; reduce heat and simmer about 1 hour. Add carrots, turnip, and celery. Continue to cook until meat and vegetables are tender, about 45 minutes. Remove meat and vegetables and keep warm. Skim off excess fat. Measure 1 cup cooking liquid. Melt margarine; stir in flour; add cooking liquid and bouillon cube. Gradually add milk and horseradish. Bring mixture to boiling point and cook 2 minutes, stirring constantly. Serve sauce with sliced beef and vegetables.

Sjömansbiff

Norwegian sailor's stew

4 servings

 1½ pounds round steak, cut into
   8 thin slices
 3 tablespoons margarine or
   butter
 3 medium onions, sliced
 8 medium potatoes, sliced
 1 teaspoon salt
 ⅛ teaspoon black pepper
 1 pint light ale

Brown steak slices in hot margarine; remove and keep warm. Saute onions in remaining margarine until transparent and lightly browned; sprinkle with salt and pepper. Place alternate layers of meat, onions, and potatoes in a heavy saucepan. Pour the pan drippings from meat and onions over layers. Add ale. Cover and simmer gently until potatoes are tender about 1½ hours.

Slottsstek

Swedish pot roast

6 servings

 3½–4 pounds rump beef roast
 1 teaspoon salt
 ¼ teaspoon black pepper
 2 tablespoons oil
 1¼ cups beef bouillon
 2 medium onions, chopped
 4 anchovy fillets, chopped
 1 bay leaf
 5 peppercorns
 8 allspice berries
 2 tablespoons vinegar
 1 tablespoon molasses
 ½ cup heavy cream
 2 tablespoons flour

Rub beef with salt and pepper. In a heavy, large saucepan, brown beef on all sides in oil. Add bouillon, onion, anchovies, bay leaf, peppercorns, allspice, vinegar, and molasses. Cover and cook over low heat about 2 hours, or until meat is tender. Remove meat and strain pot liquid. Stir flour and cream into liquid. Cook, stirring constantly, until thickened. Serve gravy with sliced pot roast.

Skinkstek

Swedish roast fresh ham

4 to 6 servings

$\frac{1}{2}$ *fresh ham*
1 *teaspoon salt*
$\frac{1}{2}$ *teaspoon black pepper*
1 *teaspoon ground ginger*
1 *teaspoon rosemary*
1 *beef bouillon cube*
1$\frac{1}{4}$ *cups boiling water*

Score top of ham in diamond pattern. Rub ham with salt, pepper, ginger, and rosemary. Place ham on rack in roasting pan. Roast in a moderate oven (350°) about 2 hours, allowing 30 to 35 minutes per pound. Remove all but 2 tablespoons of pan juices. Add bouillon cube dissolved in boiling water. Stir to mix with meat juices. Serve gravy with sliced roast.

Fläskkotletter

Swedish pork chops

4 servings

1 *teaspoon salt*
$\frac{1}{2}$ *teaspoon black pepper*
$\frac{1}{2}$ *teaspoon ground ginger*
2 *tablespoons flour*
4 *($\frac{1}{2}$" thick) loin pork chops*
2 *tablespoons oil*

Mix salt, pepper, ginger, and flour. Dust chops with mixture. In a heavy skillet, brown chops lightly on both sides in hot oil. Lower heat and cook until done, about 20 minutes.

Fläskkarré

Swedish loin of pork

4 to 6 servings

3 *pounds loin of pork*
10 *prunes*
1$\frac{1}{4}$ *cups water*
1 *teaspoon salt*
$\frac{1}{4}$ *teaspoon black pepper*
$\frac{1}{2}$ *teaspoon ginger*
2 *tablespoons flour*

With a sharp knife, make an opening the length of the roast. Cover prunes with water; bring to a boil. Cool. Reserve liquid. Remove prune pits. Rub opening in meat with salt, pepper, and ginger. Insert cooked prunes in opening; secure opening with skewers. Place meat in open roasting pan. Roast in a moderate oven (350°) about 1 hour and 30 to 45 minutes. Remove meat. Pour off all but 3 tablespoons pan drippings. Stir in flour. Slowly add 1$\frac{1}{4}$ cups liquid from prunes. Stir over low heat until thickened and smooth. Serve gravy with sliced pork.

Kinkku

Finnish roast fresh ham

4 servings

$\frac{1}{2}$ *fresh ham*
1 *teaspoon salt*
$\frac{1}{4}$ *teaspoon pepper*
1 *medium tart apple, sliced*
1 *medium onion, chopped*
10 *cooked prunes, pitted*
1 *tablespoon chopped parsley*
1 *bouillon cube*
1 *cup boiling water*

Score top of ham in diamond pattern. Cut large pocket in meat directly under the top, cutting from the side. Sprinkle meat and inside of pocket with salt and pepper. Combine apple, onion, prunes, and parsley; fill cavity. Fasten opening with wooden picks or skewers. Place ham in roasting pan and roast in moderate oven (350°) allowing 30 to 35 minutes per pound. Remove meat and keep warm. Pour off excess fat. Stir bouillon and boiling water into pan and blend with pan juices. Serve gravy with slices of meat.

According to legend, dishes such as Swedish hash and collops (photo below) originated on small ships, where the cooks had little equipment available and had to do their utmost to serve a nourishing daily meal.

Pytt i panna

Swedish hash

4 servings

>   2 medium onions, chopped
>   2 tablespoons margarine or
>   butter
>   2 cups diced, cooked beef or
>   pork
> 4–5 medium potatoes
>   cooked, peeled and diced
>   1 teaspoon salt
> ¼ teaspoon black pepper
>   4 fried eggs
>   1 tablespoon chopped parsley

In a large heavy skillet, sauté onions in margarine until golden and transparent. Add diced meat, potatoes, salt and pepper. Cook until mixture is lightly browned. Top each serving with a fried egg; sprinkle with parsley.

Kalops

Swedish collops

6 servings

>   3 pounds beef for stew
>   1 teaspoon salt
> ¼ teaspoon black pepper
> ¼ cup flour
>   3 tablespoons salad oil
>   2 medium onions, chopped
>   2 bay leaves
>   1 (1 pound) can whole
>   cranberry sauce

Sprinkle meat with salt and pepper. Dredge meat with flour. Heat oil in Dutch oven; brown meat in oil on all sides. Add onions, bay leaves and cranberry sauce; stir. Cover. Cook over medium heat, stirring occasionally, until meat is tender about 1½ hours.

Cabbage and lamb go together naturally, and the two straight-forward flavors complement each other to perfection. (Recipe page 58, 1st column).

Får i kål

Lampaanpaisti

Stekt lammsaddel

Norwegian lamb and cabbage stew

6 servings

2 tablespoons salad oil
3 pounds lamb with bone, cut into 2″ pieces
1 (2 pound) head of cabbage
2 teaspoons salt
2 beef bouillon cubes
2 cups hot water
1 bay leaf
Chopped parsley

Heat oil in Dutch oven. Brown meat in oil until well browned; remove meat; discard drippings. Wash and trim cabbage; separate into leaves. Place alternate layers of cabbage and meat in Dutch oven. Sprinkle each layer with salt. Add bouillon cubes, water, and bay leaf. Bring to a boil; reduce heat. Cover. Simmer about 1½ hours or until meat is tender. Remove bay leaf. Sprinkle with parsley before serving.

Finnish lamb steaks

4 servings

2 tablespoons salad oil
1 clove garlic, minced
1 teaspoon crushed rosemary
1 teaspoon salt
¼ teaspoon black pepper
4 (½″ thick) lamb steaks

Combine oil, garlic, rosemary, salt and pepper; rub on both sides of lamb steaks. Let lamb steaks stand at least 3 hours. Broil, 3 inches from heat, until brown on one side, about 8 minutes; turn and broil same time on other side.

Norwegian crown of lamb

6 servings

1 (5–6 pound) crown roast of lamb
1 tablespoon lemon juice
1 tablespoon salad oil
2 pounds ground lamb
1 clove garlic, minced
1 tablespoon chopped parsley
1 teaspoon grated lemon rind
1 teaspoon salt
¼ teaspoon black pepper

Have the bones of the roast "Frenched" that is remove tails from the end bones leaving bones bare. Rub outside of crown with lemon juice and then oil. Combine ground lamb, garlic, parsley, lemon rind, salt and pepper. Place meat mixture inside crown. Pat down firmly and round top. Place on a rack in roasting pan. Bake in a moderate oven (350°) about 1½ hours or to desired degree of doneness. Turn off heat and leave in oven 10 minutes. Place crown on serving plate. Put paper frills on rib bones, if desired. Carve like a pie.

Hökarpanna

Swedish kidney hash

4 servings

- 1 *pound beef kidneys*
- 4 *tablespoons margarine or butter*
- 1 *pound boneless pork, slivered*
- 2 *onions, thinly sliced*
- 6 *medium potatoes, peeled and thinly sliced*
- 1 *teaspoon salt*
- ¼ *teaspoon black pepper*
- 1 *(12 ounce) bottle beer or ale or*
- 1½ *cups beef bouillon*

Remove fat and white veins from kidney; wash; dry with paper towel. Slice kidneys thinly. Melt margarine in large skillet; brown pork and kidneys in margarine. Add onions; cook until transparent. Add potatoes, salt and pepper. Stir in beer. Cook over medium heat, stirring occasionally, until meat is cooked, about 45 minutes.

Benlöse fugle

Danish beef and ham birds

6 servings

- 6 *(½" thick) slices round steak*
- 1 *(4-ounce) package Canadian bacon*
- 6 *tablespoons flour*
- ½ *teaspoon salt*
  Dash black pepper
- 2 *tablespoons salad oil*
- 1 *medium onion, chopped*
- 2 *cups beef bouillon*
- ⅓ *cup water*

Pound beef slices until slightly flattened. Place bacon on beef slices; roll up and secure with wooden toothpicks. Combine flour, salt and pepper. Dredge meat rolls with flour; save flour. Heat oil in large heavy skillet. Brown meat on all sides in oil. Add onion; cook until transparent. Stir in bouillon Cover. Simmer 1½ hours or until meat is tender. Remove meat; keep warm. Mix remaining flour with water; add to pan liquids. Cook stirring constantly until thickened. Serve gravy over meat.

Ugnstekt kotlettrad

Swedish roast pork

4 servings

- 1½ *teaspoons powdered ginger*
- 1 *teaspoon salt*
- ¼ *teaspoon black pepper*
- ½ *teaspoon dried sage*
- 3 *pounds pork rib roast*

Combine ginger, salt, pepper and sage; rub into pork. Place pork in shallow roasting pan. Bake in a moderate oven (350°) until meat is tender about 1½ hours.

Kalvkyckling

Swedish veal rollettes

8 servings

- 8 *slices ham 6" × 4" × ⅛"*
- 8 *thin veal cutlets, ⅛" thick*
- 4 *tablespoons margarine or butter*
- ½ *cup aquavit or dry white wine*
- 1 *(8 ounce) package processed Swiss cheese, shredded*

Place ham slices on veal; roll up and secure with wooden toothpicks. Melt margarine in large heavy skillet over medium heat. Brown meat on all sides in margarine. Add aquavit. Cover. Cook over medium heat until meat is tender about 8 to 10 minutes. Remove; keep warm. Add cheese. Cook over low heat, stirring constantly, until cheese is melted. Serve sauce over veal rolls.

Dill (shown here in Finnish dill meat) is an age-old Scandinavian herb. Its name comes from the Anglo-Saxon 'dillan,' meaning 'to fall asleep.' In olden times dill extract was taken as a harmless sleeping potion, and according to an ancient popular belief the bride who put a twig of dill in her shoe would be assured of a mild-tempered husband.

Swedish roast pork (recipe: page 59, 3rd column)

Tilliliha

Finnish dill meat

6 servings

3	pounds boneless lamb, cut into 1½″ pieces
3½	cups water
2	teaspoons salt
1	teaspoon dill weed
10	peppercorns, crushed
1	bay leaf
½	cup flour
¼	cup dry red wine
	Fresh dill or parsley, optional

Place meat in Dutch oven. Add 3 cups of water, salt, dill, peppercorns, and bay leaf. Bring just to a boil; reduce heat. Cover; simmer 1½ hours or until meat is tender. Mix flour and remaining water; stir into meat. Add wine. Continue to cook, stirring constantly until thickened about 3 to 5 minutes. Garnish with chopped dill or parsley.

Tender lamb from southern Finland is unrivalled in quality, and it is one of Finland's favorite national dishes.

Lammasmuhennos

Finnish lamb stew

6 servings

   3 *pounds boneless lamb, cubed*
   6 *potatoes, sliced*
   4 *carrots, cut into 1" pieces*
   2 *leeks, cut into ½" pieces*
   1 *teaspoon salt*
 ¼ *teaspoon black pepper*
   3 *cups water*
   1 *tablespoon chopped parsley*

Place alternate layers of meat and vegetables in large Dutch oven. Sprinkle each layer with salt and pepper. Add water. Bring to a boil; reduce heat. Cover. Simmer 1½ hours or until meat is tender. Sprinkle with parsley before serving.

Poultry and game dishes

In the enjoyable book by Selma Lagerlöf, that tells the story of the fantastic travels of young Nils Holgersson, the little Swedish boy rides through the country on the back of a wild goose. Each year the geese return in their V-formation against the blue sky, and their long cry echoes in the stillness of the Swedish forest. They are on their way to Lapland in the far north. Other animals, which have disappeared from almost all the rest of Europe, still live in the woods of Sweden, Norway and Finland. The bear and the elk are two examples. These animals are protected by law, and each year only a carefully restricted number can be killed. In Swedish and Finnish restaurants a leg of bear sometimes appears on the menu. It is a dark brown, slightly tough meat with an adventurous and wild flavor. Vast herds of reindeer roam the frozen tundra of the far north, and reindeer is a Scandinavian delicacy. Cold reindeer served with a compote of arctic berries belongs in any festive smörgåsbord. Reindeer tongue in jelly with sour cream is among the most delicious snacks of famous gourmet restaurants. Another gourmet dish is the unique pâté which the chef can make from the snow grouse of Lapland.

Stekt gås

Swedish roast goose

8 servings

      1 (12 pound) goose
    ½ lemon
      1 teaspoon salt
    ¼ teaspoon black pepper
      8 apples, cored and quartered
    30 pitted prunes
      2 teaspoons caraway seed
      2 tablespoons cornstarch
      2 cups chicken bouillon

Wash and dry goose. Remove any excess fat inside cavity. Rub neck and body cavities of goose lightly with lemon, salt, and pepper. Fill cavities with apples, prunes and caraway seed. Skewer openings shut. Place on rack in shallow roasting pan, breast side down. Roast in a slow oven (325°) about 4 to 4½ hours, or until tender when pierced with a fork and juices are light yellow, not pink. Drain fat during roasting. Remove goose; keep warm. Skim off fat from pan drippings. Mix cornstarch and bouillon; add to pan. Cook over medium heat, stirring and scraping browned bits, until thickened. Discard stuffing. Serve gravy with goose.

Gåsfett

Goose fat

Place excess fat from cavity of goose in a small saucepan. Cover with water. Bring to a boil; continue to boil until fat melts. Remove from heat; strain through cheesecloth into small bowl. When fat solidifies, pour off water. Use for frying or bread baking.

Sort gryte

Norwegian black pot

6 servings

> 1 (10½ ounce) can cream of
>   mushroom soup
> 1 cup milk
> ½ teaspoon salt
> ½ teaspoon black pepper
> 2 cups cooked, diced chicken
> 1 cup cooked, diced ham
> 1 (10 ounce) package frozen
>   peas
> 2 leeks, cooked and cut into
>   ½″ pieces
> 4 tomatoes, peeled and
>   quartered
> ¼ cup Madeira wine

In a large saucepan, combine
soup, milk, salt and pepper;
blend well. Heat. Stir in chicken,
ham, peas, leeks and tomatoes.
Cook, stirring occasionally,
until heated about 10 minutes.
Stir in wine. Serve with
cornbread, if desired.

Stekt kyckling

Swedish roast chicken

6 servings

> 4 tablespoons margarine or
>   butter
> 1 onion, chopped
> 1 cup chopped celery
> ½ cup chopped dried apricots
> 1 teaspoon salt
> ½ teaspoon thyme
> ¼ teaspoon sage
> 2 chicken bouillon cubes
> ⅓ cup water
> 6 slices (3 cups) white bread,
>   cubed
> 1 (5 pound) roasting chicken

Melt margarine in large skillet;
sauté onion and celery until
onion is transparent. Stir in
apricots, salt, thyme, sage,
bouillon cubes and water. Heat
to boiling, crushing bouillon
cube. Remove from heat. Add
bread cubes; toss lightly until
evenly moistened. Wash chicken
and pat dry. Stuff neck and body
cavities lightly with stuffing.
Skewer openings closed. Place
chicken on rack in shallow
roasting pan. Roast in a
moderately hot oven (375°)
about 2½ hours or until
drumstick moves easily at joint.
Thicken pan drippings if desired.

Kokt höns

Swedish chicken

6 servings

> ¼ cup margarine or butter
> 6 boned chicken breasts
> ½ cup dry white wine
> 2 tablespoons gin
> 1 teaspoon dill weed
> ½ teaspoon powdered thyme
> ½ teaspoon salt

Melt margarine in large skillet
over medium heat. Brown
chicken in margarine. Add wine,
gin, dill, thyme and salt. Cover.
Simmer about 20 minutes or
until chicken is tender.

Kanipaisti

Finnish rabbit fricassee

4 servings

> 6 slices bacon, diced
> 1 (2½ pound) package frozen
>   rabbit, thawed
> 2 chicken bouillon cubes
> 1 cup hot water
> 2 tablespoons flour
> ½ teaspoon salt
> 1 cup heavy cream
> 1 tablespoon red currant jelly

In large skillet, fry bacon until
crisp; remove. Drain off fat;
return ¼ cup fat to skillet.
Brown rabbit on both sides.
Dissolve bouillon cubes in
water; pour over rabbit. Cover.
Cook over medium heat until
rabbit is tender, about 45
minutes. Remove rabbit; keep
warm. Stir flour and salt into
cream. Gradually stir cream into
pan liquid. Cook, stirring
constantly, until thickened. Stir
in jelly until melted. Add bacon.
Pour gravy over rabbit.

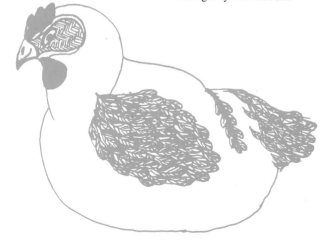

Sweet desserts

Because canned fruit has become so convenient, the full, rich flavor of dried fruit tends to be forgotten. But on distant and isolated farms in Scandinavia, apples, plums and pears that have ripened during the summer are dried and used in preparing delicious sweet dishes throughout the long winter.

Kräm på torkad frukt

Swedish dried fruit cream

4 to 6 servings

    1 (12 ounce) package mixed
       dried fruit
    4 cups water
    2 tablespoons sugar
    ½ teaspoon ground mace
    2 tablespoons cornstarch
    3 tablespoons water

Simmer fruit in water until tender, about 15 minutes. Stir in sugar and mace. Mix cornstarch with cold water; add to fruit mixture. Cook over medium heat, stirring constantly, until thickened. Stir carefully to avoid breaking up fruit. Chill. Serve cold plain, with cream or with soft or baked custard.

'Light and airy like a summer's cloud' – Swedish whipped farina is a popular dessert, especially with youngsters.

Norwegian rice porridge (recipe: page 66, 1st column)

Klappgröt

Swedish whipped farina

6 servings

2½ cups water
  1 (6 ounce) can frozen
       concentrate for punch
  4 tablespoons farina

In a saucepan, combine water and punch concentrate; bring to a boil. Sprinkle farina into boiling mixture; stir vigorously. Simmer over low heat until farina is cooked, about 5 minutes. Pour mixture into 1½-quart bowl. Beat with an egg beater or hand electric mixer for about 1 minute at a time, at intervals of about 5 minutes, until pudding is fluffy and cool. Chill. Serve with milk or cream if desired.

Risgrynsgröt

Norwegian rice porridge

4 to 6 servings

> 3 cups cooked rice
> 4½ cups milk
> 1 tablespoon margarine or
>   butter
> ⅛ teaspoon salt
> 2–3 tablespoons sugar

In a large heavy saucepan,
combine well drained rice with
milk. Cook, covered, over low
heat until milk is absorbed;
stir occasionally. Stir in
margarine, salt and sugar. Chill.
Serve with cream or apple
compote.

Bärkräm

Swedish berry cream

6 to 8 servings

> 1 pint fresh strawberries,
>   raspberries, blueberries or
>   gooseberries (mixture)
> 2½ cups water
> 2 tablespoons sugar
> 3 tablespoons cornstarch
> 3 tablespoons water

Rinse berries. In a large
saucepan, combine berries and
water; simmer over medium heat
2 to 3 minutes. Stir in sugar.
Blend cornstarch and water into
a smooth paste. Add cornstarch
to berries, stirring constantly.
Bring mixture to a boil; cook
3 minutes. Chill.

Rödgröd med flöde

Norwegian fruit jelly with cream

4 servings

> 1 pint red currants
> 1 pint raspberries
> 2 cups water
> ½ cup sugar
> 1 tablespoon cornstarch
> 2 tablespoons water
> 1 teaspoon vanilla extract

In a large saucepan, rinse fruit.
Combine fruit and water;
simmer over medium heat about
10 minutes. Drain; stir in sugar.
Blend cornstarch and water into
a smooth paste. Add cornstarch
to fruit, stirring constantly.
Bring mixture to a boil; cook
3 minutes. Remove from heat
and stir in vanilla. Sieve mixture,
if desired. Chill. Serve with
cream and decorate with
blanched almonds, if desired.

Rabarberkräm

Swedish rhubarb cream

4 to 6 servings

> 4 cups rhubarb, peeled and cut
>   into 1½" pieces
> 2 cups water
> ¼ cup sugar
> 3 tablespoons cornstarch
> 3 tablespoons water

In a large saucepan, combine
rhubarb and water; cook over
medium heat until tender. Stir in
¼ cup sugar and taste; add
more sugar if desired. Blend
cornstarch and water into a
smooth paste. Add cornstarch
to fruit, stirring constantly.
Bring mixture to a boil; cook
3 minutes; cool. Chill well
before serving.

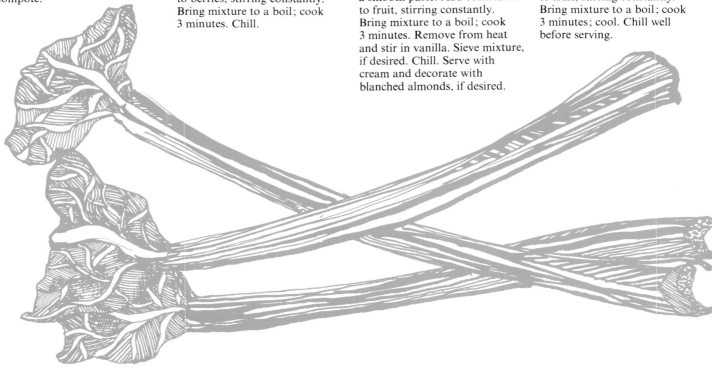

Karamellpudding

Norwegian caramelcream

6 to 8 servings

    2 cups sugar
    3 tablespoons boiling water
    3 egg yolks
    2 tablespoons sugar
    1 cup milk
    1 teaspoon vanilla extract
    ½ cup heavy cream
    3 cups applesauce page 67

In cast-iron skillet or heavy saucepan, melt sugar over very low heat; stir until completely melted and golden brown. Remove from heat. Carefully add boiling water to melted sugar; stir mixture until well blended. Combine egg yolks and 2 tablespoons of sugar, milk and vanilla in top of double-boiler. With wire-whip, beat mixture until foamy; cook until hot. Beating constantly, (do not use electric mixer) add melted sugar, now cooled to "soft-ball" stage to custard mixture. Continue to beat until mixture cooks. Remove from heat and continue beating until mixture has cooled completely. Beat cream and fold into cooled custard mixture. Chill. Serve cold over applesauce.

Aeblegröd

Danish applesauce

6 to 8 servings

    2 pounds apples, peeled, cored
      and cubed
    ¼ cup water
    2 tablespoons white wine
    1 tablespoon sugar

In a large saucepan, cook apples with water until just tender; stir in wine. Mash, do not sieve. Add sugar and taste; add more sugar if desired. Chill.

Kan ikke lade vaere

Danish lemon delight

12 servings

    10 eggs, separated
    1 cup sugar
    1 envelope unflavored gelatin
    ½ cup water
    ½ cup lemon juice

Beat egg yolks and sugar together with electric mixer until well blended. Sprinkle gelatin over water in small saucepan. Place saucepan over low heat. Cook until gelatin is melted about 2 to 3 minutes. Let cool slightly, then beat gradually into egg yolk mixture. Beat in the lemon juice. In a large bowl, beat egg whites until stiff; fold into yolk mixture. Pour into a glass bowl. Chill until set.

Vaniljsås

Swedish custard

4 to 6 servings

    3 egg yolks
    ¼ cup sugar
    1½ cups heavy cream
    1 teaspoon vanilla extract

In top of double boiler over boiling water, beat egg yolks, sugar, 1 cup heavy cream and vanilla. Cook until thick, beating constantly. Remove from heat; stir vigorously until the custard is cool. Whip remaining half cup of cream; fold into custard. Chill.

The pancake is a Swedish specialty, the perfect dessert on a chilling winter's day.

Swedish crisp pancakes

Ugnspannkaka

Swedish baked pancake

8 to 10 servings

  2 eggs
2½ cups milk
 ½ teaspoon salt
  2 teaspoons sugar
1½ cups sifted flour

In a medium bowl, beat eggs with 1 cup of the milk until well blended. Stir in salt, sugar and flour to make a smooth batter. Stir in remainder of milk; blend until smooth. Set batter aside for 10 minutes. Butter a 12″ × 8″ × 2″ baking dish. Stir batter and pour into prepared pan. Bake in a hot oven (400°) for 30 minutes or until pancake is golden brown and puffy. Serve immediately with jam or fruit purée.

Apples grow the world over, but each country makes its own special filling for baked apples. Delicate, bittersweet almond-flavored filling blends deliciously with sweet Scandinavian apples.

Fraspannkakor

Swedish crisp pancakes

4 servings

  2 *eggs, separated*
1¼ *cups water*
  ¼ *teaspoon salt*
  1 *tablespoon sugar*
  1 *cup sifted all-purpose flour*
  ½ *cup heavy cream, whipped*
  1 *tablespoon margarine or*
     butter

In a medium bowl, beat egg yolks, water, salt, sugar and flour until well blended. Fold in whipped cream. Beat egg whites until stiff; fold into batter. Rub a crêpe pan or small skillet lightly with margarine. Add 3 to 4 tablespoons batter; tip pan and let batter spread over the bottom. Cook over medium heat just until bubbles appear on surface. Turn; cook until browned. Serve with puréed fruit if desired.

Mandelfyllda stekta äpplen

Swedish baked apples with almond filling

6 servings

  1 *cup ground almonds*
  ¼ *cup sugar*
  ¼ *cup water*
  2 *egg whites*
  6 *baking apples*
  2 *tablespoons margarine or*
     butter, melted
  ½ *cup dried bread crumbs*

In an electric blender, combine almonds, sugar, water, unbeaten egg whites; blend to a smooth paste. Set aside. Peel apples and core almost to the bottom. Brush apples with melted margarine and roll in bread crumbs. Fill cored apples with the almond paste. If any margarine, bread crumbs or almond paste remain, spread on top of apples. Place apples, sides just touching, in 8″ or 9″ pie pan. Bake in a moderate oven (350°) 30 to 40 minutes, or until apples test fork-tender. Serve with custard page 67.

Bondepige med slör

Danish veiled country lass

8 servings

- ¼ cup margarine or butter
- 4 cups pumpernickel bread, finely crumbled
- 2 tablespoons sugar
- 3 cups applesauce
- 1 cup heavy cream, whipped
- ½ cup raspberry jam or jelly

Melt margarine in large skillet; stir in bread crumbs, fry until crisp. Stir in sugar until well blended; set aside. In bottom of pretty glass bowl, layer ⅓ of bread mixture. Cover with 1½ cups applesauce. Top applesauce with second ⅓ of bread mixture; top with remaining 1½ cups applesauce. Top second layer of applesauce with remaining bread mixture. Top with layer of whipped cream. Make 8 pools in whipped cream; fill each pool with raspberry jam or jelly. Chill.

Aeblekage

Danish apple cake

4 to 6 servings

- 2 tablespoons sugar
- ½ teaspoon vanilla
- 1 (16 ounce) can applesauce
- 1¼ cups dried bread crumbs
- ½ cup melted margarine or butter
- 1 cup cream, whipped
  Jelly

Add sugar and vanilla to applesauce. Butter an ovenproof dish; alternate layers of bread crumbs, and applesauce ending with bread crumbs. Pour melted margarine over all. Bake in a very hot oven (450°) about 25 to 30 minutes. Serve hot topped with whipped cream and jelly.

Klatkage

Finnish rice fritters

4 servings

- 1 cup cooked rice, cold
- 2 eggs
- 2 tablespoons raisins
- ¼ teaspoon grated lemon rind
- 2 tablespoons chopped almonds
- 2–3 tablespoons flour
- 4 tablespoons margarine or butter
  Powdered sugar
  Jam or jelly

Combine rice, eggs, raisins, lemon rind, almonds and flour. Form mixture into small cakes. Melt margarine in skillet; fry cakes in margarine on both sides. Sprinkle with powdered sugar and serve with jam or jelly.

Arme riddere

Norwegian poor knights

4 servings

- 2 eggs
- ½ cup milk
- 8 slices white bread, without crusts
- ¼ cup dried bread crumbs
- 2 tablespoons sugar
- 2 teaspoons cinnamon
- 2 tablespoons margarine or butter
  Jam, jelly or powdered sugar

Beat eggs and milk; dip bread slices in mixture. Combine bread crumbs, sugar, and cinnamon. Sprinkle on each side of bread slices. Heat margarine on griddle; sauté bread slices on both sides until golden brown. Spread with jam or jelly or sprinkle with powdered sugar before serving.

Riskrem

Danish rice pudding

6 servings

    3 cups milk
   ½ cup rice or
    2 cups pre-cooked rice
   ½ teaspoon vanilla
   ¾ cup sugar
    2 envelopes gelatine
   ¼ cup cold water
   ¼ cup chopped almonds
    4 tablespoons margarine or
      butter
    1 cup heavy cream, whipped

Bring milk to a boil. Add rice,
vanilla and sugar. Simmer over
medium heat until cooked, or if
instant rice is used, cover and
let stand 5 minutes over lowest
heat. Remove from heat and stir
in gelatin softened in ¼ cup
cold water. Stir in almonds and
margarine. Cool. Fold in
whipped cream. Pour into a
2-quart mold; chill until set.
Unmold and serve cold.

Brylépudding

Swedish caramel mold

6 servings

    1 cup sugar
    6 eggs
    2 cups light cream
   ½ teaspoon vanilla
   ½ cup cream, whipped
    2 tablespoons brandy

In a heavy pan, melt ½ cup of
the sugar over very low heat
until just golden brown. Pour
into bottom of a 9″ ring
mold; spread to cover entire
bottom. Beat eggs well; add
½ cup sugar, cream and vanilla.
Pour into mold. Set mold in a
pan of hot (not boiling) water;
bake in a moderate oven (325°)
1 hour or until knife inserted in
center comes out clean. Cool.
Dip mold quickly into a pan of
hot water and unmold. Whip
cream and brandy together until
soft peaks form. Serve over
molded dessert.

Pastries

Lucia gingersnaps (below right) and country lasses (below left), recipe page 74, 4th column.

Lucia-pepparkakor

Swedish Lucia gingersnaps

3 dozen

1 (14½-ounce) package
 gingerbread mix
⅓ cup lukewarm water
⅛ teaspoon lemon extract

Blend ingredients. Chill dough.
Roll dough out on floured
board. Cut into desired shape.
Place on buttered cookie sheet
and bake in moderately hot
oven (375°) 8 to 10 minutes.

Gräddtårta

Kinuskikakku

Swedish cream cake

8 servings

  3 *9" sponge cake layers*
    page 77, 2nd column
  1 *cup applesauce or jam*
1½ *cups prepared packaged*
    vanilla pudding
  2 *cups heavy cream*
 ½ *teaspoon vanilla*
  2 *tablespoons sugar*
20 *strawberries*

Spread one cake layer with ½ of the applesauce or jam, then ½ of the pudding. Place second layer on top; spread with remaining applesauce and pudding. Top with third layer. Whip cream; add vanilla and sugar. Spread cream over cake; garnish with strawberries.

Finnish caramel-iced cake

10 servings

  1 *recipe caramel icing*
 ¾ *cup margarine or butter*
  1 *chiffon cake, page 75,*
    4th column
  3 *tablespoons lemon juice*
  3 *tablespoons water*
  2 *tablespoons chopped*
    pistachio nuts

Prepare caramel icing according to directions; cool. Cream margarine until fluffy; blend into icing. Slice the cake horizontally into 3 equal layers. Combine lemon juice and water; sprinkle over each layer. Spread top of each layer with icing, and stack. Ice top layer and sides. Sprinkle with pistachio nuts.

Caramel icing:
 ¾ *cup sugar*
1½ *cups cream*
  5 *teaspoons cocoa*
  5 *teaspoons dark molasses*

In saucepan, combine all ingredients. Cook over low heat until mixture forms a soft ball in cold water. Cool slightly before using.

Kronans kaka

Swedish crown cake

4 servings

- 2 eggs
- ½ cup granulated sugar
- ¼ cup margarine or butter
- ⅔ cup ground almonds
- 2 boiled, cold medium potatoes, grated
- 2 tablespoons bread crumbs

In a bowl, beat the eggs and sugar until thick and foamy. In another bowl, cream margarine, add ground almonds, then gradually add egg mixture. Blend well; add potatoes. Grease an 8-inch cake pan and sprinkle with bread crumbs shaking off excess crumbs. Pour batter into pan. Bake in a moderate oven (350°) 25 minutes. Cool. Serve cake with lemon sauce, if desired.

Marstrandskex

Marstrand cookies

6 dozen cookies

- 1 cup potato flour
- 1¾ cups flour
- 2 teaspoons baking powder
- 1 cup granulated sugar
- 1 cup heavy cream
- 1 cup melted margarine or butter

In a bowl, sift together the flours, and baking powder. Add sugar, cream and margarine; knead quickly. Chill dough until firm. Roll dough thinly, about ⅛″ thick; prick in several places with a fork. With a pastry cutter, cut out cookies of about 2½″ in diameter. Bake cookies on buttered cookie sheet in a moderate oven (350°) about 10 minutes, or until very lightly browned.

Bruna bröd

Swedish brown spice cookies

5 dozen cookies

- 1¾ cups flour
- 1 teaspoon baking powder
- ½ cup brown sugar
- ½ cup finely chopped almonds
- 1 teaspoon cinnamon
- 1 teaspoon ground cardamom
- 1 cup, plus 2 tablespoons soft margarine or butter
- 1 egg yolk
  Granulated sugar

In a large bowl mix all ingredients except granulated sugar. Knead quickly; chill. Shape dough into a long roll ½″ wide. Cut off small pieces of dough and roll into balls; dip into granulated sugar. Bake cookies on a buttered cookie sheet in a moderately hot oven (375°) about 12 minutes.

Bondkakor

Swedish country lasses

5 dozen cookies

- 2 cups flour
- 1½ teaspoons baking powder
- ¾ cup sugar
- ¾ cup coarsely chopped almonds
- 1 tablespoon molasses
- ⅔ cup margarine or butter

In a large mixing bowl, blend all ingredients; knead to make a smooth, firm dough. Divide dough into 3 parts; roll into cylinders, about 1½″ in diameter. Refrigerate until firm Cut cylinders into ¼″ slices. Bake on a greased cookie sheet in a hot oven (400°) about 10 minutes.

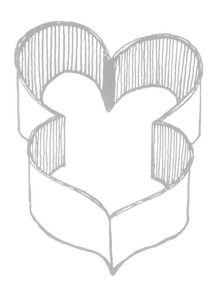

Finska pinnar

Finnish shortbread

4 dozen cookies

2½ cups flour
½ cup sugar
¼ cup finely chopped almonds
¾ cup margarine or butter,
    softened
1 egg, slightly beaten
2 tablespoons sugar
    Coarsely chopped almonds

Combine flour, sugar, almonds
and margarine; knead into a
firm dough. (If necessary, add a
few drops of water to make
dough easy to handle.) Use
about 1 teaspoonful of dough for
each cookie. Roll dough into a
log about 2″ long. Dip in
egg, then in sugar and chopped
almonds. Bake on buttered
cookie sheet in a hot oven (400°)
about 10 minutes.

Semlor

Bread and almond filled buns

10 buns

1 recipe plain buns, page 77
¼ cup cream or milk
¾ cup ground almonds
⅔ cup sugar
    Confectioner's sugar

Prepare recipe for buns; cool.
Cut a lid from each bun and
remove inside crumbs. Soak
crumbs in cream or milk. Mix
almonds and sugar with soaked
crumbs. Fill buns; replace lids.
Heat in moderate oven (350°)
for a few minutes. Sprinkle with
confectioner's sugar.

Fyllda bullar

Almond filled buns

10 buns

1 recipe plain buns, page 77
½ cup almond paste
1 cup heavy cream, whipped
    Confectioner's sugar

Prepare recipe for buns; cool.
Blend almond paste and whipped
cream. Let stand in refrigerator
at least one hour. Stir. Cut a lid
from each bun, and make a
small cavity; fill with almond
mixture. Replace lids and
sprinkle with confectioner's
sugar. Serve immediately. (If not
used immediately, filled buns
should be refrigerated.)

Englekake

Norwegian chiffon cake

8″ or 9″ tube cake

1 cup cake flour
1½ teaspoons baking powder
¾ cup sugar
½ teaspoon salt
¼ cup vegetable oil
2 egg yolks
4 tablespoons orange juice
1 teaspoon grated orange rind
4 egg whites
¼ teaspoon cream of tartar

In a large mixing bowl, sift flour,
baking powder, sugar and salt.
Make a well in center; pour in
oil, egg yolks, orange juice and
rind. Beat with electric mixer
2 minutes until satiny smooth.
Beat egg whites and cream of
tartar until stiff. Add batter to
egg whites a little at a time,
gently folding in with rubber
spatula until evenly blended. *Do
not beat.* Pour in ungreased 8″
or 9″ tube pan. Bake in a slow
oven (325°) 35 minutes; then
increase heat to 350° and bake
until top springs back when
pressed lightly with finger (about
5 minutes). Invert until cold.
Loosen from sides with knife and
remove carefully.

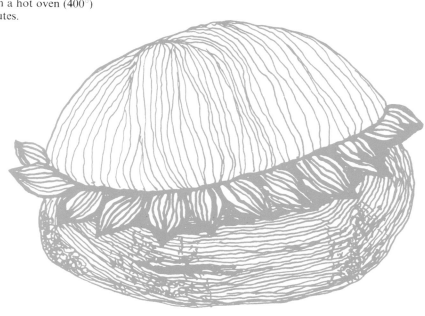

Smaland is a land of rich green pastures, producing sweet cream in abundance. Small wonder, then, that the Smaland farmer's wife makes Scandinavia's smoothest and sweetest cottage cheese and cream cakes.

Swedish plain buns

Småländskostkaka

Swedish cheese cake

8 servings

  2 cups cottage cheese
¼ cup flour
  3 eggs
¼ cup sugar
  2 cups light cream
½ cup coarsely chopped
    almonds, lightly toasted

Stir cottage cheese by hand or with mixer, until granular. Add flour, eggs, sugar, cream, and almonds; mix well. Grease a 10″ fluted pie pan or 8″ square baking pan. Pour in mixture; bake in a moderate oven (350°) 50 to 60 minutes, or until knife inserted in center comes out clean.
Garnish with whipped cream and jelly.

*Danish pastries in an early stage
of their preparation, and (below)
ready for serving (recipe page 78)*

77

Släta bullar

Swedish plain buns

10 buns

>   2 packages dry yeast
>   1 cup light cream
>   1 cup margarine or butter
> ¼ cup sugar
> ¼ cup ground almonds
>   1 teaspoon ground cardamom
> 3¼ cups flour
>   1 egg
>   Beaten egg

Blend yeast and ½ cup of the
cream. Melt margarine. Add
remaining ½ cup cream and heat
mixture until lukewarm; add to
yeast. Stir in sugar, ground
almonds, cardamom, half of the
flour, and egg. Add remaining
flour gradually, stirring
constantly. Knead dough until
smooth. Sprinkle a little flour on
top, cover with a cloth and
allow dough to rise until double
in size. Turn dough onto a
lightly-floured surface; knead
until smooth again. Divide
dough into 10 equal pieces and
shape into round, smooth buns
without cracks. Place buns on
greased baking sheet; let rise
until doubled. Brush carefully
with beaten egg. Bake in hot
oven (400°) for 10 minutes.

Sokerikakku

Finnish light sponge cake

1 layer or 1 small tube cake

>   1 cup cake flour
> 1¼ teaspoons baking powder
>   Pinch of salt
>   2 eggs, separated
> ¾ cup sugar
> ¼ cup hot water
> ½ teaspoon vanilla

Sift together flour, baking
powder and salt. Beat egg whites
until they stand in soft peaks.
Gradually beat in ¼ cup of the
sugar. Add hot water and vanilla
to egg yolks; beat until thick.
Beat in remaining ½ cup sugar.
Pour egg yolks over whites,
cutting and folding until well
blended. Fold in flour mixture.
Spoon batter into unbuttered
9″ layer or 7- or 8″ tube
pan. Bake in a moderate oven
(350°) 20 to 30 minutes, or until
cake springs back when pressed
lightly with finger. Invert on
wire cake rack; let stand until
cold. Loosen edges with sharp
knife; ease out of pan.

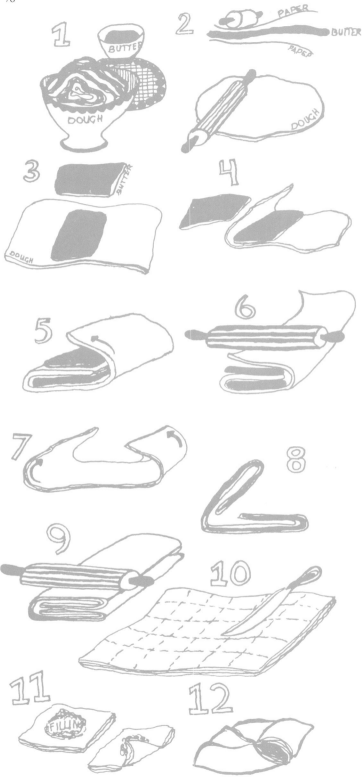

Wienerbröd

Danish pastries

40 pastries

1¼ cups cold butter
½ cup flour
2 envelopes dry yeast
½ cup warm water
½ cup cold milk
¼ cup sugar
1 egg, beaten
3¼ cups flour

Filling:

1 cup almonds or hazelnuts
1¼ cups confectioner's sugar
2 egg whites or
1 lightly-beaten egg

Chop together cold butter and ½ cup flour; knead until mixture sticks together. Refrigerate to harden. Dissolve yeast in warm water; add cold milk. Stir in sugar, egg, and half the flour. Gradually add remaining flour, stirring constantly. Knead dough until smooth and shiny; set aside. Roll butter mixture between wax paper into an oblong about 7″ × 14″. Place on cookie sheet; refrigerate. Roll out dough on lightly floured board into a square about 14″ × 14″. Place butter oblong over half of the dough, remove wax paper, and fold other half over it. Press lightly with rolling pin; roll doubled dough in the other direction into oblong strip. Fold dough into 3 sections— fold one edge in ⅓ of the way, then the other. Roll again into an oblong. Repeat the rolling and folding twice more. (In all, dough should be rolled and folded 3 times.) Flour board between rolling, and brush off any surplus flour from dough. If dough shows a tendency to become sticky, discontinue the rolling and refrigerate 10 to 15 minutes or until dough becomes firm. After third rolling and folding, cover dough with a clean towel; refrigerate for 15 minutes. Grind nuts. Add the confectioner's sugar; stir in enough egg white or beaten egg to make mixture smooth and stiff. Make pastries into desired shapes, crescents, bow knots, braids, etc., using about 1 teaspoon nut filling on each. Place pastries on buttered baking sheets and let stand about 15 minutes in a cool place. Bake in a hot oven (400°) about 15 minutes. Cool. If desired, drizzle with confectioner's glaze.

Kransekager

Frasvåfflor

Äggvåfflor

It may be because of the long, dark winter that keeps people indoors, but Scandinavian baking, which requires hours of devotion, has achieved a level unsurpassed anywhere in the world. The most delicious things emerge from the oven. Wheat and rye bread come in the most fantastic forms: round, flat, oval, braided and ring-shaped. The variations in sweet cakes are even more incredible, not only for festive holidays, but for breakfast and coffee time, in fact sweet cakes for every minute of the day. Swedish cakes in particular are often heavily flavored with such Eastern spices as ginger and cardamon. The tradition was probably inherited from the adventurous Vikings, who voyaged along the great rivers of Russia to reach Constantinople, and returned heavily laden with priceless Eastern spices. The finest Danish cake is of course 'Wienerbröd', or 'Viennese rolls' (but what we know as Danish pastries), made from paperthin, crispy, light layers of dough. Danish bakers apparently learned to prepare this buttery yeast dough from the Viennese. But in Vienna itself people call Wienerbröd 'Copenhagen pastries', and it is the unique quality of famous Danish butter that gives this cake its incredible lightness.

Danish almond cakes

25 cakes

1⅔ cups ground almonds
1¼ cups sugar
3 egg-whites, lightly beaten
   Confectioner's sugar

In a saucepan, combine almonds, sugar and egg-whites. Beating vigorously, simmer the mixture slowly over low heat until it thickens and retains its shape. Remove from heat and cool. Divide dough into 25 equal pieces; shape into small loaves about 2½" long. Roll loaves in confectioner's sugar. Press gently to make the tops pointed. Bake on a buttered cookie sheet, lightly sprinkled with flour, in a hot oven (400°) about 6 minutes. The cakes should set on the surface and brown lightly but remain soft inside.

Swedish cream waffles

4 servings

1¼ cups flour
1 cup cold water
¼ teaspoon salt
¼ cup melted margarine or
   butter
1¾ cups heavy cream

In a bowl, mix flour, water, salt and margarine into a smooth batter. Whip cream until stiff; fold into batter. Chill batter about 1 hour. Heat waffle iron; brush lightly with a little melted margarine. Pour batter into center of lower half until it spreads about 1" from edges. Bring cover down gently. Bake at medium heat until waffle iron stops steaming. Serve immediately with sugar, jam or fruit.

Swedish egg waffles

4 servings

1 cup all purpose flour
1 teaspoon baking powder
2 eggs, separated
1¼ cups heavy cream
¼ cup melted margarine or
   butter

In a large bowl, combine flour and baking powder. In a small bowl, beat egg yolks with cream; add to flour. Blend until smooth. Stir in margarine. Beat egg whites until stiff but not dry; carefully fold into batter. Heat waffle iron; brush lightly with a little melted margarine. Pour batter into center of lower half until it spreads about 1" from edges. Bring cover down gently. Bake at medium heat until waffle iron stops steaming. Serve immediately with sugar, jam or whipped cream if desired.

Candies

Knäck

Swedish toffee

Makes 64-1" squares

    1 cup sugar
    ¾ cup heavy cream
    ¾ cup molasses
    ⅓ cup chopped almonds
    4 tablespoons margarine or
       butter

In a heavy saucepan, combine sugar, cream, and molasses. Cook over moderate heat until candy reaches hard ball stage, 248° F. on the candy thermometer. Add almonds and margarine; stir to mix. Pour into an 8" square pan. Cool. Cut into 1" squares.

Suklaakakku

Finnish chocolate ice

48 pieces

    1 (6-ounce) package
       semi-sweet chocolate pieces
    3 tablespoons margarine or
       butter
    1 egg
    1 tablespoon grated orange
       peel

Melt chocolate with margarine in top of double boiler; cool slightly. Beat egg in a small bowl with electric mixer. Slowly add chocolate and orange peel; beat until thoroughly blended. Drop from teaspoon onto a buttered cookie sheet. Chill thoroughly until firm.

Chokladkola

Chocolate toffee

Makes 64–1" squares

    2 cups sugar
    1 cup dark corn syrup
    1 cup evaporated milk
    3 (1-ounce) squares
       unsweetened chocolate, cut
       into small pieces
    1 tablespoon margarine
       or butter
    1 teaspoon vanilla

In a heavy saucepan, combine sugar, corn syrup, milk, and chocolate pieces. Cook over moderate heat until mixture reaches the hard ball stage, 248° F. on a candy thermometer. Stir constantly. Add margarine and vanilla; stir well. Pour candy into a buttered 8" square pan. Do not scrape the sides of the pan. When partially cooled, mark into 1" squares. When thoroughly cooled, cut into squares and wrap individually in waxed paper.

Tjinuskikola

Tjinuski caramels

Makes 64–1" squares

    1½ cups sugar
    ¼   cup cocoa
    ⅓   cup molasses
    1¾ cups milk
    ¼   cup margarine or butter
    1   teaspoon vanilla

In a heavy saucepan, combine sugar, and cocoa. Add molasses, milk and margarine. Cook over moderate heat, stirring constantly, until candy reaches hard ball stage, 248° F. on a candy thermometer. Pour into buttered 8" square pan. Do not scrape the sides of pan. When partially cooled, mark and cut into 1" squares. When thoroughly cooled, wrap individually in waxed paper.

Beverages

Glögg

Swedish glogg

8 servings

1 (26-ounce) bottle dry red
  wine or
1 (26-ounce) bottle aquavit
1 cup sugar
1 stick cinnamon
5 cloves
6 cardamom seeds, crushed
1 orange peel spiral
½ cup slivered almonds
½ cup raisins

Combine wine, sugar, cinnamon,
cloves, cardamom and orange
peel in saucepan; stir to blend.
Let stand 3 to 4 hours. Heat, but
do not boil. Light with a match
and pour burning into heatproof
cups containing a few almonds
and raisins.

Vinbowle

Danish wine cooler

12 servings

2 orange slices
1 lemon, sliced
¼ cup sugar
¼ cup brandy
  Ice
1 (26-ounce) bottle dry white
  wine, chilled
1 (12-ounce) bottle club
  soda, chilled

Place fruit in tall pitcher;
sprinkle with sugar. Press fruit
with back of spoon to release
flavor. Add brandy. Chill 1 to 2
hours. Add ice and wine; stir to
blend. Add club soda just before
serving.

Saftglögg

Fruit juice glogg

6 servings

2 cups apple juice
1 cup grape juice
2 tablespoons sugar
1 stick cinnamon
4 cloves
1 orange peel spiral
⅓ cup raisins
⅓ cup slivered almonds

In saucepan, combine juices,
sugar, spices and orange peel
spiral; bring just to a boil.
Place several raisins and almonds
in punch cups. Remove cloves,
cinnamon and orange peel
spiral from juice; pour into cups.

Mumma

Swedish mumma

4 to 5 servings

  1 (12-ounce) bottle dark
      beer, chilled
  1 (12-ounce) bottle light
      beer, chilled
  1 (12-ounce) bottle ale, chilled
  ¼ cup gin

Combine all ingredients in a
large well chilled pitcher; stir to
blend. Serve immediately.

Julglögg

Swedish Christmas punch

12 servings

  2 cups aquavit
  1 (26-ounce) bottle dry red
      wine
  ½ cup sugar
  1 cinnamon stick
  5 cloves
  4 cardamom seeds, crushed
  1 orange peel spiral
  ½ cup slivered almonds
  ½ cup raisins

Combine aquavit, wine, sugar,
spices and orange peel in
saucepan. Heat but do not boil.
Light with a match and pour
burning into glögg glasses or
heat-proof cups containing a
few almonds and raisins.

Eggedosis

Norwegian eggcream

Makes 1 quart

  10 egg yolks
  ½ cup sugar
  1 cup brandy
      Nutmeg

Beat egg yolks and sugar
together until thick and
creamy, about 5 to 7 minutes.
Gradually add brandy; beat
until well blended. Pour into
punch bowl or individual
punch cups. Sprinkle with
nutmeg.

Traditional Christmas dishes

Dark and sad are the last weeks of the year in Scandinavia. The cloudy, snowy sky gives only a dim gray light which slowly, almost unnoticeably slides into darkness as early as four in the afternoon. Dead stillness reigns in the limitless woods, and the lakes and the sea itself are frozen. It makes Scandinavians all the happier to withdraw into their own houses by cozy fires, and to warm themselves from within with heart-warming food and drink. For as long as people have been living in this northernmost part of Europe, the days when the sun is at its lowest and all of nature lies under the dead stillness of a blanket of snow, have been a time for staying indoors. Before Christianity arrived in the land, the winter solstice, the moment late in December when the days begin to lengthen again, was a celebrated event. Later, many of the ancient, heathen traditions of the solstice feast were made a part of the Christian Christmas. Today, be it in Norway, Sweden, Denmark, or Finland, Christmas is a feast of light and warmth in the house, of crackling logs in the fireplace, of flickering candles in the Christmas tree and wreaths, of warmth and pleasure and of groaning tables that all but collapse under the weight of the food heaped on them. Baking begins weeks in advance, and different kinds of breads, often in the ancient, traditional forms of wreaths and sun rays are a particular speciality. In remote farms people brew Christmas beer and distill akvavit. Lutfish go into their wooden tubs and pigs and geese are killed. And when the great season arrives on Christmas Eve, the table is finally laid for twelve days of feasting. Traditional Christmas dishes are lutfish and rice porridge, ham, braised goose filled with apples and served with red cabbage, liver paté, spicy sausages, head cheese and cookies and cakes without end. The Norwegians are fond of spareribs served with sauerkraut; the Danes always expect goose; the Swedes and the Finns prefer ham, braised and prepared in a pastry shell. For drink there is foamy beer or Glögg, a steamy, hot concoction made with wine, brandy or akvavit, and fragrant spices. In Norway it is served with thin pancakes made from rye flour and wrapped around slices of goat cheese.

The delicacies crammed into the store room of a Scandinavian farmhouse – freshly brewed beer, home-baked loaves of bread, chimney-smoked sausages and hams, sweet butter and marinated fish. All of them are on display in abundance during the festive Christmas season.

Christmas dishes

Sildesalat

Danish herring salad

6 servings

1 *(1 pound) jar pickled schmaltz herring, meat removed from bones, cut into ½″ cubes*
4 *medium, diced, cooked potatoes*
1 *cup diced pickled beets*
1 *cup diced dill pickle*
2 *medium tart apples, peeled and diced*
1 *tablespoon finely chopped onion*
  Dash white pepper
½ *cup sour cream*
½ *teaspoon salt*
  Lettuce leaves

Combine all ingredients. Taste and add salt, if needed; chill. Serve cold on lettuce leaves, garnished, if desired, with parsley and sliced hard-cooked egg.

Leverpastej

Swedish liver paté

2 loaves

1 *pound pork liver*
1 *quart water*
1 *tablespoon salt*
1 *pound bacon*
4 *anchovy fillets*
1 *teaspoon margarine or butter*
1 *tablespoon finely chopped onion*
½ *teaspoon salt*
1 *teaspoon white pepper*
3 *eggs*
1 *tablespoon cornstarch*
2 *tablespoons cold water*
2 *cups heavy cream*
¼ *pound bacon slices, if desired*

In 2-quart bowl, soak liver in water and salt about 2 to 3 hours; drain. Put liver through fine blade of meat grinder, alternating with 1 pound bacon strips and anchovies. In small skillet melt margarine; sauté onion in margarine until transparent. Add salt, pepper, eggs, cornstarch mixed with water, and cream. Beat with fork until smooth. Line two 9″ × 5″ × 3″ loaf pans with greased aluminum foil or slices of bacon. Put 3½ cups mixture into each pan; cover with aluminum foil. Place pans in large baking pan; fill to a depth of 1″ with hot water. Bake in a moderate oven (350°) about 1 hour or until knife inserted near center shows no pink meat or juices. Chill well. Unmold. Serve in slices on bread or lettuce leaves.

Leverpastej i gelé

Liver paté in aspic

2 loaves

1 *recipe liver paté page 86*
4 *beef bouillon cubes*
3 *cups boiling water*
4 *envelopes unflavored gelatin*
1 *cup cold water*
2 *hard-cooked eggs, sliced*

Prepare liver paté, chill well; unmold. Remove bacon slices, if used. Dissolve bouillon cubes in boiling water. Soften gelatin in cold water; dissolve in hot bouillon. Pour about ⅛″ gelatin mixture into each 9″ × 5″ × 3″ loaf pan. Arrange egg slices in an attractive pattern in gelatin. Allow to chill in refrigerator or over ice cubes until set. Place liver paté on layer of eggs and gelatin. Pour remaining gelatin mixture over and around paté. Cover and chill until firm, at least 4 hours. Loosen carefully, dip into hot water, unmold onto serving platter.

Kalvsylta

Swedish jellied veal

10 to 12 servings

1 *(4 to 4½ pound) shoulder, neck, breast, rump or leg of veal with bone*
9 *cups water*
1 *tablespoon salt*
10 *peppercorns*
5 *allspice berries*
1 *bay leaf*
2 *cloves*
1 *medium onion, peeled and quartered*
2 *tablespoons vinegar*
4 *envelopes unflavored gelatin*
1 *cup cold water*

Place meat in 6 to 8 quart saucepan. Cover with water; add salt, peppercorns, allspice, bay leaf, cloves and onion. Cover, bring to a boil; reduce heat; simmer 1½ hours or until meat is loosened from bones. Remove meat; allow to cool. Remove bones and gristle, return to bouillon and simmer gently another hour. Dice meat and set aside (about 2½ cups). Strain bouillon; measure and if necessary, add water to make 7 cups. Return to saucepan. Correct seasonings. Stir in vinegar. Bring just to a boil; reduce heat; simmer. Soften gelatin in cold water; dissolve in the hot broth. Chill in refrigerator or over ice cubes, stirring frequently, until consistency of thick egg white. Stir in reserved diced meat. Pour into 2 loaf pans or 1½ quart molds which have been rinsed with cold water. Chill until firm. Unmold.

Delikatessköttbullar

Swedish delicatessen meatballs

50 to 75 meatballs

½ *pound ground beef*
½ *pound ground veal*
¼ *pound ground pork or sausage*
1 *teaspoon salt*
¼ *teaspoon white pepper*
1 *egg yolk*
½ *cup fine dry bread crumbs*
1 *cup half-and-half*
1 *tablespoon chopped onion*
¼ *cup margarine or butter Flour*

Combine meats, salt, pepper, egg yolk, crumbs and cream; mix well with fork. Cook onion in 1 tablespoon of the margarine until transparent; mix into meat mixture. Form small meat balls with two teaspoons; roll in flour. In large frying pan over moderately high heat, brown meat balls on all sides in remaining margarine. Drain on paper towels.

Rödkål

Norwegian red cabbage

6 servings

2 *tablespoons margarine or butter*
2 *pounds red cabbage, finely shredded*
2 *medium apples, peeled and sliced*
1 *medium onion, chopped*
2 *teaspoons caraway seed, crushed*
1 *teaspoon salt*
2 *tablespoons maple or dark corn syrup*
¼ *cup vinegar*
2 *tablespoons water*

In a large heavy saucepan, melt margarine. Add cabbage, apples, onion, caraway seed, salt, syrup, vinegar and water. Cover; bring to a boil, tossing lightly occasionally to blend. Reduce heat and simmer about 45 minutes or until tender. Stir occasionally; add a little water, if needed. Remove cover during last 10 minutes to allow any excess liquid to evaporate. Serve with Christmas ham, roast goose or duck.

Brunkål

Norwegian braised red cabbage

4 to 6 servings

4 *tablespoons margarine or butter*
2 *pounds red cabbage, finely shredded*
2 *tablespoons sugar*
1 *tablespoon lemon juice*
¾ *cup cranberry juice cocktail*
1 *tart apple, peeled, cored and grated*

Melt margarine in a non-metallic saucepan. Add cabbage; sauté 2 to 3 minutes, tossing lightly. Add sugar, lemon juice, cranberry juice and apple. Cover and simmer for about 1 hour or until tender, stirring occasionally.

Griljerad skinka

Swedish Christmas ham

6 servings

> 1 (3-pound) canned ham
> 1 egg, lightly beaten
> 2 tablespoons prepared
>   mustard
> 1 tablespoon sugar
> 2 tablespoons fine, dry bread
>   crumbs
> 4 tablespoons water
> 2 tablespoons tart jelly
>   (crabapple, red currant, or
>   seedless raspberry)

Place ham in baking pan. Bake
in a moderate oven (325°) for
1 hour. Remove from oven;
increase temperature setting to
400°. Mix together the egg,
mustard and sugar; spread over
ham; sprinkle with bread
crumbs. Return to oven about
10 minutes or until crumbs are
golden brown. Place on warm
platter; let rest about 10
minutes before carving.
Meanwhile, add water to
contents of baking pan; stir and
scrape until all brown bits are
loosened. Bring to a boil. Strain
into a small saucepan. Add jelly,
heat until jelly melts. Serve hot
or cold with hot or cold sliced
ham.

Kokta grisfötter

Swedish boiled pig's feet

4 servings

> 2 fresh pig's feet (about 1¼
>   pounds) washed and cut
>   in half lengthwise
>   Cold water
> 2 tablespoons salt
> 1 quart water
> 8 white peppercorns
> 8 allspice berries

Place pig's feet in large bowl
with water to cover. Cover and
place in refrigerator for 12 hours
or overnight. Rinse. Place in
2-quart saucepan. Cover with
cold water, bring to a boil; pour
off water. Add salt, 1 quart
water and spices to pig's feet in
saucepan. Cover, bring to a boil,
reduce heat; cook about 2½
hours or until bones are
loosened. Pour off liquid. Rinse.
Serve with mustard and pickled
beets.

Kinkku

Finnish ham

12 to 14 servings

>   1 (12 to 14 pound) fresh ham
> ½ cup salt
>   2 tablespoons sugar
>   1 tablespoon saltpetre
> 10 quarts water
>   8 cups coarse or Kosher salt
>   3 tablespoons dehydrated
>   horseradish
>   6 cups rye flour
> 1–1½ cups water
>   Bread crumbs

Rub ham all over with mixture
of salt, sugar and saltpetre.
Cover lightly with plastic wrap.
Refrigerate 2 days. Combine
water, coarse salt and
horseradish; bring to a boil.
Cool. Place ham in extra large
bowl, crock or plastic pail or
basket; pour in cooled salted
water. Make sure ham is
completely covered by water.
Let stand in very cool place 8 to
10 days. Remove ham; rinse in
cold water; pat dry with paper
towel. Mix together flour and
water; roll or pat out into large
square 18″ × 18″. Cover ham
with dough. Place ham on rack
in shallow roasting pan. Bake in
a moderate oven (350°) for
5 hours. Remove crust; sprinkle
ham with bread crumbs. Return
to oven. Bake 10 minutes or
until crumbs are browned and
crisp.

No one knows how old the Swedish tradition of eating lutfisk at Christmas is. The custom may date back as long ago as the Vikings, and it certainly has its roots in the time before the Reformation when it was traditional to fast before Christmas and eat only fish on Christmas Eve. The preparation of lutfisk (the name means 'lye fish') is very complicated, and the housewife must begin her work in the first week of December. The fish, usually dried cod, is first sawed into pieces and then soaked in a wooden tub in which the water is changed every day. A layer of lime is then sprinkled into the bottom of the tub, the fish is laid on the lime, more lime is sprinkled on top and then covered with a soda solution. A wide plank and a weight are placed on top of the fish, which is left to stand for six days. (In other parts of Scandinavia the process is even more complicated: instead of a soda solution a birchwood broth is used.) Finally the fish must soak for another week in fresh water changed every day. Then the lutfisk can be cooked (always wrapped in a towel) and served as the central dish at the festive Christmas dinner together with potatoes and cream sauce.

Alongside the Christmas tree, the pine branches and pine cones, the wreaths and red ribbons which all decorate Swedish homes during the darkest days of the year, the sweet and spicy gingerbread house is always present. It stands there in all its glossy brown sweetness as the symbol of domestic happiness. The gingerbread house is always prepared by the children of the family (but with the expert help of the mother, of course). The mother prepares the dough, which is rolled out to a thin layer. Then the parts of the house are cut out using cardboard forms and the individual pieces are baked in the oven. When the walls and roof forms have been cooled on a rack, they are decorated with colored glaze from a pastry bag: the doors and windows get borders, there are piles of 'snow' for the roof, and decorated paper curtains are hung in the windows. Then the house is put together, with the cardboard forms used as supports. What happier scene can there be than the little gingerbread house, set deep in the snow, a small mirror representing a nearby frozen lake, and pine branches simulating the snow-laden trees surrounding the house.

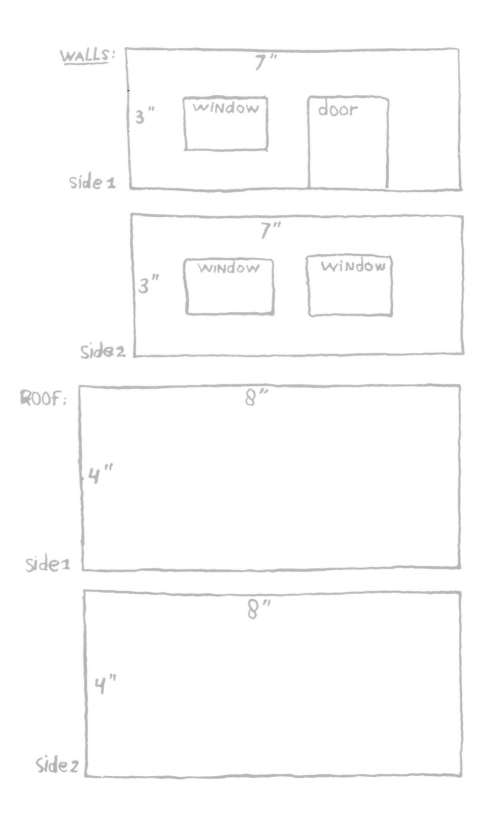

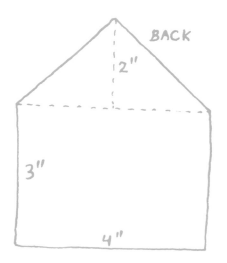

BACK

2"

3"

4"

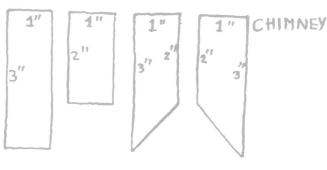

1"   1"   1"   1"   CHIMNEY

2"   2"   2"

3"   3"   3"

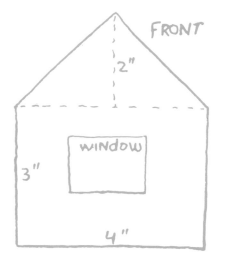

FRONT

2"

3"

window

4"

Pepparkakshus

Gingerbread house

1 house

> 1 cup brown sugar, firmly
>   packed
> 1 cup molasses
> 1 cup shortening
> 5 cups sifted flour
> 1 tablespoon baking soda
> 1 tablespoon cinnamon
> 1 tablespoon ground ginger

Place brown sugar, molasses and shortening in large saucepan. Cook over medium heat, stirring frequently, until well blended. Sift together flour, baking soda, cinnamon and ginger; stir into warm molasses mixture until well blended. While dough is still warm, remove about one quarter of the dough; knead in hands to shape into a fine-grained ball. Roll out on lightly floured surface to a rectangle about $\frac{1}{8}$" thick and large enough to cut out pieces needed. Repeat with remaining dough until all pieces of the house are cut out. Place carefully on greased cookie sheet. Bake in a moderately hot oven (375°) until edges barely begin to brown and surface is no longer puffy, about 5 to 8 minutes. Remove carefully to racks; cool.

To make gingerbread house:
Cut out – as indicated in drawing – and bake:
2 pieces (3 × 7") for walls. Cut out windows and door as indicated in drawing.
2 pieces (4 × 8") for roof.
2 pieces (4 × 5") for front and back. Cut out edges and window, as indicated in drawing.
4 pieces (1 × 3", 1 × 2" and 2 pieces 1 × 3") for chimney. Cut off edges as indicated in drawing.

Decorate sides and roof with frosting to outline windows, doors, roof tiles, window boxes etc.; let dry. Spread frosting on ends of sides and on roof pieces where they meet; assemble chimney. Put house together; place chimney on top. Let stand until firm.

Frosting:
> 1 egg white
> 2 cups sifted confectioners'
>   sugar
> 1 teaspoon lemon juice

Place all ingredients in small deep mixing bowl. Beat at high speed until firm. It should be of a soft enough consistency to flow through a fine pastry tube to make the decorations, but stiff enough to hold its shape. While mixing, add a few drops more lemon juice or a tablespoon more or less of sugar, to obtain this consistency. Decorate Gingerbread House.

Conversion tables

Liquid measures

American
standard cup | **metric equivalent** (approximately)

1 cup = ½ pint = 8 fl. oz. (fluid ounce) = 2,37 dl (deciliter)
1 tbs. (tablespoon) = ½ fl. oz. = 1,5 cl (centiliter)
1 tsp. (teaspoon) = ⅙ fl. oz. = 0,5 cl
1 pint = 16 fl. oz. = 4,73 dl
1 quart = 2 pints = 32 fl. oz. = 9,46 dl

British
standard cup | **metric equivalent** (approximately)

1 cup = ½ pint = 10 fl. oz. = 2,84 dl
1 tbs. = 0.55 fl. oz. = 1,7 cl
1 tsp. = ⅕ fl. oz. = 0,6 cl
1 pint = 20 fl. oz. = 5,7 dl
1 quart = 2 pints = 40 fl. oz. = 1,1 l (liter)

1 cup = 16 tablespoons
1 tablespoon = 3 teaspoons

1 liter = 10 deciliter = 100 centiliter

Oven temperatures

Centigrade	Fahrenheit	
up to 105° C	up to 225° F	cool
105–135° C	225–275° F	very slow
135–160° C	275–325° F	slow
175–190° C	350–375° F	moderate
215–230° C	400–450° F	hot
230–260° C	450–500° F	very hot
260° C	500° F	extremely hot

Solid measures

American/British | **metric equivalent** (approximately)

1 lb. (pound) = 16 oz. (ounces) = 453 g (gram)
1 oz. = 28 g
2.2 lbs. = 1000 g = 1 kg (kilogram)
3½ oz. = 100 g

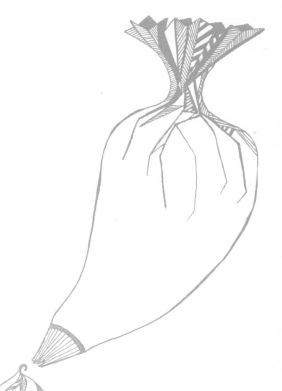

Kitchen terms

Aspic
A stiff gelatine obtained by combining fish or meat bouillon with gelatine powder.

Au gratin
Obtained by covering a dish with a white sauce (usually prepared with grated cheese) and then heating the dish in the oven so that a golden crust forms.

Baste
To moisten meat or other foods while cooking to add flavor and to prevent drying of the surface. The liquid is usually melted fat, meat drippings, fruit juice or sauce.

Blanch (precook)
To preheat in boiling water or steam. (1) Used to inactivate enzymes and shrink food for canning, freezing, and drying. Vegetables are blanched in boiling water or steam, and fruits in boiling fruit juice, sirup, water, or steam. (2) Used to aid in removal of skins from nuts, fruits, and some vegetables.

Blend
To mix thoroughly two or more ingredients.

Bouillon
Brown stock, conveniently made by dissolving a bouillon cube in water.

Broth
Water in which meat, fish or vegetables have been boiled or cooked.

'En papillote'
Meat, fish or vegetables wrapped in grease-proof paper or aluminum foil (usually first sprinkled with oil or butter, herbs and seasonings) and then baked in the oven or grilled over charcoal. Most of the taste and aroma are preserved in this way.

Fold
To combine by using two motions, cutting vertically through the mixture and turning over and over by sliding the implement across the bottom of the mixing bowl with each turn.

Fry
To cook in fat; applied especially (1) to cooking in a small amount of fat, also called sauté or pan-fry; (2) to cooking in a deep layer of fat, also called deep-fat frying.

Marinate
To let food stand in a marinade usually an oil–acid mixture like French dressing.

Parboil
To boil until partially cooked. The cooking is usually completed by another method.

Poach
To cook in a hot liquid using precautions to retain shape. The temperature used varies with the food.

Reduce
To concentrate the taste and aroma of a particular liquid or food e.g. wine, bouillon, soup, sauce etc. by boiling in a pan with the lid off so that the excess water can evaporate.

Roast
To cook, uncovered, by dry heat. Usually done in an oven, but occasionally in ashes, under coals or on heated stones or metals. The term is usually applied to meats but may refer to other food as potatoes, corn, chestnuts.

Sauté
To brown or cook in a small amount of fat. See Fry.

Simmer
To cook in a liquid just below the boiling point, at temperatures of 185°–210°. Bubbles form slowly and collapse below the surface.

Skim
To take away a layer of fat from soup, sauces, etc.

Stock
The liquid in which meat or fish has been boiled together with herbs and vegetables.

Whip
To beat rapidly to produce expansion, due to incorporation of air as applied to cream, eggs, and gelatin dishes.

Alphabetical index

Scandinavian

Index by type of dish